THE MAIDENS' LODGE

None of Self and All of Thee,
(in the Reign of Queen Anne)

EMILY SARAH HOLT

1st WORLD
LIBRARY
Literary Society

The Maidens' Lodge

Emily Sarah Holt

© 1st World Library, 2007
PO Box 2211
Fairfield, IA 52556
www.1stworldlibrary.com
First Edition

LCCN: 2007930742

Softcover ISBN: 978-1-4218-4818-1
Hardcover ISBN: 978-1-4218-4721-4
eBook ISBN: 978-1-4218-4915-7

Purchase *"The Maidens' Lodge"*
as a traditional bound book at:
www.1stWorldLibrary.com/purchase.asp?ISBN=978-1-4218-4818-1

1st World Library is a literary, educational organization
dedicated to:

- Creating a free internet library of downloadable ebooks

- Hosting writing competitions and offering book publishing
scholarships.

Interested in more 1st World Library books? contact:
literacy@1stworldlibrary.com
Check us out at: www.1stworldlibrary.com

1st World Library Literary Society

Giving Back to the World

"If you want to work on the core problem, it's early school literacy."

- James Barksdale, former CEO of Netscape

"No skill is more crucial to the future of a child, or to a democratic and prosperous society, than literacy."

- Los Angeles Times

"Literacy... means far more than learning how to read and write... The aim is to transmit... knowledge and promote social participation."

- UNESCO

"Literacy is not a luxury, it is a right and a responsibility. If our world is to meet the challenges of the twenty-first century we must harness the energy and creativity of all our citizens."

- President Bill Clinton

"Parents should be encouraged to read to their children, and teachers should be equipped with all available techniques for teaching literacy, so the varying needs and capacities of individual kids can be taken into account."

- Hugh Mackay

CHAPTER ONE

PHOEBE ARRIVES AT WHITE-LADIES

"The sailing of a cloud hath Providence to its pilot."

Martin Farquhar Tupper.

In the handsome parlour of Cressingham Abbey, commonly called White-Ladies, on a dull afternoon in January, 1712, sat Madam and her granddaughter, Rhoda, sipping tea.

Madam—and nothing else, her dependants would have thought it an impertinence to call her Mrs Furnival. Never was Empress of all the Russias more despotic in her wide domain than Madam in her narrow one.

As to Mr Furnival—for there had been such a person, though it was a good while since—he was a mere appendage to Madam's greatness—useful in the way of collecting rents and seeing to repairs, and capable of being put away when done with. He was a little, meek, unobtrusive man, fully (and happily) convinced of his own insignificance, and ready to sink himself in his superb wife as he might receive orders. He had been required to change his name as a condition of alliance with the heiress of Cressingham, and had done so with as much readiness as he would in similar circumstances have changed his coat. It was about fourteen years since this humble individual had ceased to be the head servant of Madam; and it was Madam's wont to hint, when she condescended to refer to him at all, that her marriage with him had been the one occasion in her life wherein she had failed to act with her usual infallibility.

It had been a supreme disappointment to Madam that both her children were of the inferior sex. Mrs Catherine to some extent resembled her father, having no thoughts nor opinions of her own, but being capable of moulding like wax; and like wax her mother moulded her. She married, under Madam's orders, at the age of twenty, the heir of the neighbouring estate—a young gentleman of blood and fortune, with few brains and fewer principles—and died two years thereafter, leaving behind her a baby daughter only a week old, whom her careless father was glad enough to resign to Madam, in order to get her out of his way.

The younger of Madam's daughters, despite her sister's passive obedience, had been the mother's favourite. Her obedience was by no means passive. She inherited all her mother's self-will, and more than her mother's impulsiveness. Much the handsomer of the two, she was dressed up, flattered, indulged, and petted in every way. Nothing was too good for Anne, until one winter day, shortly after Catherine's marriage, when the family assembled round the breakfast table, and Anne was found missing. A note was brought to Madam that evening by one of Mr Peveril's under-gardeners, in which Anne gaily confessed that she had taken her destiny into her own hands, and had that morning been married to the Reverend Charles Latrobe, family chaplain to her brother-in-law, Mr Peveril. She hoped that her mother would not be annoyed, and would receive her and her bridegroom with the usual cordiality exhibited at weddings.

Emily Sarah Holt

Madam's, face was a study for a painter. Had Anne Furnival searched through her whole acquaintance, and selected that one man who would be least acceptable at Cressingham, she could not have succeeded better.

A chaplain! the son of a French Huguenot refugee, concerned in trade!—every item, in Madam's eyes, was a lower deep beyond the previous one. It was considered in those days that the natural wife for a family chaplain was the lady's maid. That so mean a creature should presume to lift his eyes to the sister of his patroness, was monstrous beyond endurance. And a Frenchman!—when Madam looked upon all foreigners as nuisances whose removal served for practice to the British fleet, and boasted that she could *not* speak a word of French, with as much complacency as would have answered for laying claim to a perfect knowledge of all the European tongues. And a tradesman's son! A tradesman, and a gentleman, in her eyes, were terms as incompatible as a blue rose or a vermilion cat. For a man to soil his fingers with sale, barter or manufacture, was destructive of all pretension not only to birth, but to manners.

On the head of her innocent spouse Madam's fury had been outpoured in no measured terms. Receive the hussy, she vehemently declared, she would not! She should never set foot in that house again. From this moment she had but one daughter.

Two years afterwards, on the evening of Catherine's funeral, and of the transference of baby Rhoda to the care of her grandmother, a young woman, shabbily dressed, carrying an infant, and looking tired and careworn, made her way to the back door of the Abbey. She asked for an interview with Madam.

"I cannot disturb Madam," said the grey-haired servant, not

unkindly; "her daughter was buried this morning. You must come again, my good woman."

"Must I so, Baxter?" replied the applicant. "Tell her she has one daughter left. Surely, if ever she will see me, it were to-night."

"Eh, Mrs Anne!" exclaimed the man, who remembered her as a baby in arms. "Your pardon, Madam, that I knew you not sooner. Well, I cannot tell! but come what will, it shall never be said that I turned my young mistress from her mother's door. If I lose my place by it, I'll take in your name to Madam."

The answer he received was short and stern. "*My daughter* was buried this morning. I will not see the woman."

Baxter softened it a little in repeating it to Mrs Latrobe. But he could not soften the hard fact that her mother refused to see her. She was turning away, when suddenly she lifted her head and held out her child to him.

"Take it to her! 'Tis a boy."

Mrs Latrobe knew Madam. If a grandchild of the nobler sex produced no effect upon her, no more could be hoped. Baxter carried the child in, but he shook his grey head when he brought it back. He did not repeat the message this time.

"I'll have nought to do with that beggar tradesfellow's brats!" said Madam, in a fury.

"Mrs Anne, there's one bit of comfort," said old Baxter, in a whisper. "Master slipped out as soon as I told of you, and I saw him cross the field towards the church. Go you that way, and meet him."

Emily Sarah Holt

She did not speak another word, but she clasped the child tight to her bosom, and hurried away. As she passed a narrow outlet at the end of the Abbey Church, close to the road, Mr Furnival shambled out and met her.

"Eh, Nancy, poor soul, God bless thee!" faltered the poor father, who was nearly as much to be pitied as his child. "She'll not see thee, my girl. And she'll blow me up for coming. But that's nothing—it comes every day for something. Look here, child," and Mr Furnival emptied all his pockets, and poured gold and silver into Anne's thin hand. "I can do no more. Poor child! poor child! But if thou art in trouble, my girl, send to me at any time, and I'll pawn my coat for thee if I can do no better."

"Father," said Mrs Latrobe, in an unsteady voice, "I am sorry I was ever an undutiful child to *you*."

The emphasis was terribly significant.

So they parted, with much admiration of the grandson, and Mr Furnival trotted back to his penance; for Madam kept him very short of money, and required from him an account of every shilling. The storm which he anticipated broke even a little more severely than he expected; but he bore it quietly, and went to bed when it was over.

Since that night nothing whatever had been heard of Mrs Latrobe until four months before the story opens. When Mr Furnival was on his death-bed, he braved his wife's anger by naming the disowned daughter. His last words were, "Perpetua, seek out Anne!"

Madam sat listening to him with lips firmly set, and without words. It was not till he was past speech that she gave him any answer.

"Jack," she said at last, to the pleading eyes which were more eloquent than the hushed voice had been, "look you here. I will not seek the girl out. She has made her bed, and let her lie on it! But I will do this for you—and I should never have done that without your asking and praying me now. If she comes or sends to me, I will not refuse her some help. I shall please myself what sort. But I won't turn her quite away, for your sake."

The pleading eyes turned to grateful ones. An hour later, and Madam was a widow.

Fourteen years passed, during which Rhoda grew up into a maiden of nineteen years, always in the custody of her grandmother. Her father had fallen in one of the Duke of Marlborough's battles, and before his death had been compelled to sell Peveril Manor to liquidate his gambling debts. He left nothing for Rhoda beyond his exquisite wardrobe and jewellery, a service of gold plate, and a number of unpaid bills, which Madam flatly refused to take upon herself, and defied the unhappy tradesmen to impose upon Rhoda. She did, however, keep the plate and jewels; and by way of a sop to Cerberus, allowed the "beggarly craftsmen," whom she so heartily despised, to sell and divide the proceeds of the wardrobe.

When the fourteen years were at an end, on an afternoon in September, a letter was brought to the Abbey for Madam. Its bearer was a respectable, looking middle-aged woman. Madam ordered her to have some refreshment, while she read the letter. Rhoda noticed that her hand shook as she held it, and wondered what it could be about. Letters were unusual and important documents in those days. But it was the signature that had startled Madam—"Anne Latrobe."

Mrs Latrobe wrote in a strain of suffering, penitence, and

entreaty. She was in sore trouble. Her husband was dead; of her five children only one was living. She herself was capable of taking a situation as lady's maid—a higher position then than now—and she knew of one lady who was willing to engage her, if she could provide otherwise for Phoebe. Phoebe was the second of her children, and was now seventeen. She expressed her sorrow for the undutiful behaviour of which she had been guilty towards both parents; and she besought in all ignorance the father who had been dead for fourteen years, to plead with Madam, to help her, in any way she pleased, to put Phoebe into some respectable place where she could earn her own living. Mrs Latrobe described her as a "quiet, meek, good girl,—far better than ever I was,"—and said that she would be satisfied with any arrangement which would effect the end proposed.

For some minutes Madam sat gazing out of the window, yet seeing nothing, with the letter lying open before her. Her promise to her dead husband bound her to answer favourably. What should she do with Phoebe? After some time of absolute silence, she startled Rhoda with the question,—

"Child, how old are you?"

"Nineteen, Madam," answered Rhoda, in much surprise.

"Two years!" responded Madam,—which words were an enigma to her granddaughter.

But as Rhoda was of a romantic temperament, and the central luminary of her sphere was Rhoda Peveril, visions began to dance before her of some eligible suitor, whom Madam was going to put off for two years. She was more perplexed than ever with the next question.

"Would you like a companion, child?"

"Very much, Madam." Anything which was a change was welcome to Rhoda.

"I think I will," said Madam. "Ring the bell."

I have already stated that Madam was impulsive. When her old butler came in—a man who looked the embodiment of awful respectability—she said, "Send that woman here."

The woman appeared accordingly, and stood courtesying just within the door.

"Your name, my good woman?" asked Madam, condescendingly.

"An't please you, Molly Bell, Madam."

"Whence come you, Molly?"

"An't please you, from Bristol, Madam."

"How came you?"

"An't please you, on foot, Madam; but I got a lift in a carrier's cart for a matter of ten miles."

"Do you know the gentlewoman that writ the letter you brought?"

"Oh, ay, Mistress Latrobe! The Lord be thanked, Madam, that ever I did know her, and her good master, the Reverend, that's gone to the good place."

"You are sure of that?" demanded Madam; but the covert satire was lost on Molly Bell.

"Sure!" exclaimed she; adding, very innocently, "You can never have known Mr Latrobe, Madam, to ask that; not of late years, leastwise."

"I never did," said Madam, rather grimly. "And do you know Mrs Phoebe?"

"Dear heart, Madam!" said Molly, laughing softly, "but how queer it do sound, for sure, to hear you say Mrs Phoebe! She's always been Miss Phoebe with us all these years; and we hadn't begun like to think she was growing up. Oh, dear, yes, Madam, I knew them all—Master Charles, and Miss Phoebe, and Master Jack, and Miss Perry, and Miss Kitty."

"Miss Perry?" said Madam, in an interrogative tone.

"Miss Perpetua, Madam—we always called her Miss Perry for short. A dear little blessed child she was!"

Rhoda saw the kind which held the letter tremble again.

"And they are all dead but Miss Phoebe?"

"It's a mercy Miss Phoebe wasn't taken too," said Molly, shaking her head. "They died of the fever, in one fortnight's time—Miss Perry went the first; and then Master Jack, and then Master Charles, and the Reverend himself, and Miss Kitty last of all. Miss Phoebe was down like all of 'em, and the doctor did say he couldn't ha' pulled her through but for her dear good mother. She never had her gown off, Madam, night nor day, just a-going from one sick bed to another; and they all died in her arms. I wonder she didn't lie down and die herself at last. I do think it was Miss Phoebe beginning to get better as kept her in life."

"Poor Anne!"

If anything could have startled Rhoda, it was those two words. She recognised her aunt's name, and knew now of whom they were speaking.

Had Molly been retained as counsel for Mrs Latrobe, she could hardly have spoken more judiciously than she did. She went on now,—

"And, O Madam! when all was done, and the five coffins carried out, she says to me, Mrs Latrobe says, 'Molly,' she says, 'I'd ought to be very thankful. I haven't been a good child,' she says, 'to my father and mother. But *they'll* never pay me back my bitter ways,' she says. And I'm right sure, Madam, as Miss Phoebe never will, for she's that sweet and good, she is! So you see, Madam, Mrs Latrobe, she's had her troubles, and if so be she's sent to you for comfort, Madam, I take the liberty to hope as you'll give her a bit."

"You can go back to the kitchen, Molly," said Madam, in what was for her a very gracious tone. "I will order you a night's lodging here, and to-morrow one of my carters, who is going to Gloucester, shall take you so far on your way. I will give you a letter to carry."

"Thank you kindly, Madam!"

And with half a dozen courtesies, one for Rhoda, and the rest for Madam, Molly retreated, well pleased. Madam sat down and wrote her letter. This was Madam's letter, written in an amiable frame of mind:—

"Daughter,—I have yowr leter. Your father is ded thise foreteen yeres. I promised him as he lay a dyeing yt wou'd doe some thing for you. You have nott desarv'd itt, but I am sory to here of your troble. If you will sende youre childe to mee, I will doe so mutch for yow as too brede her upp with my granedor Roda, yowr sistar Catterin's child. I wou'd not have yow mistak my meaneing, wch is nott that shee shou'd be plac'd on a levell with her cosin, for Roada is a jantlewoman, and yt is moar than she can say. But to be Rodes wating mayd, and serve her in her chamber, and bere her cumpany when she hath need. I will give the girle too sutes of close by the yere, and some tims a shillinge in her pockit, and good lodgeing and enow of victle. And if shee be obediant and humbel, and order her self as I wou'd she may, I will besyde al this give her if shee mary her weding close and her weddying diner,—yt is, if she mary to my minde,— and if noe, thenn shee may go whissel for anie thing I will doe for her. It is moar than she cou'd look for anie whear els. You will bee a foole to say Noe.

"P. Furnival.

"Lett the girle come when you goe to your place. There is a carrer goes from Bristoll to Teukesburry, and a mann with an horse shal mete her at the Bell."

Be not horrified, accomplished modern reader, at Madam's orthography. She spelt fairly well—for a lady in 1712.

An interval of about two months followed, and then came another letter from Mrs Latrobe. She wrote in a most grateful strain; she was evidently even more surprised than pleased with the offer for Phoebe. There was a reference of penitent love to her father; a promise that Phoebe should be at Cressingham on or as near as possible to the twenty-ninth of January; and warm thanks for her mother's undeserved kindness, more especially for the consideration which had prompted the promise that Phoebe should be met at Tewkesbury, instead of being left to find her way alone in the dark through the two miles which lay between that town and Cressingham.

So, on the afternoon of that twenty-ninth of January, an hour after the man and horses had started, Madam and Rhoda sat in the Abbey parlour, sipping their tea, and both meditating on the subject of Phoebe.

Madam, as became a widow, was attired in black. A stiff black bombazine petticoat was surmounted by a black silk gown adorned with flowers in raised embroidery, and the train of the gown was pulled through the pocket-hole of the petticoat. At that time, ladies of all ages wore their dresses low and square at the neck, edged with a tucker of nett or lace; the sleeves ended at the elbows with a little white ruffle of similar material to the tucker. In London, the low head-dress was coming into fashion; but country ladies still wore the high commode, a superb erection of lace and muslin, from one to three feet in height. Long black silk mittens were drawn up to *meet* the sleeves. The shoes reached nearly to the ankles, and were finished with large silver buckles.

Rhoda was much smarter. She wore a cotton gown—for when all cotton gowns were imported from India, they were rare and costly articles—of an involved shawl-like pattern, in which the prevailing colour was red. Underneath was a petticoat of dark blue quilted silk. Her commode was brightened by blue ribbons; she wore no mittens; and her shoe-buckles rivalled those of her grandmother. Rhoda's figure was good, but her face was commonplace. She was neither pretty nor ugly, neither intellectual nor stupid-looking. Of course she wore powder (as also did Madam); but if her hair had been released from its influence, it would have been perceived that there was about it a slight, very slight, tinge of red.

The coming of her cousin was an event of the deepest

Emily Sarah Holt

interest to Rhoda, for she had been ever since her birth absolutely without any society of her own age. Never having had an opportunity of measuring herself by other girls, Rhoda imagined herself a most learned and accomplished young person. It would be such a triumph to see Phoebe find it out, and such a pleasure to receive—with a becoming deprecation which meant nothing—the admiration of one so far her inferior. Rhoda had dipped into a score or two of her grandfather's books, had picked up sundry fine words and technical phrases, with a smattering of knowledge, or what would pass for it; and she sat radiant in the contemplation of the delightful future which was to exalt herself and overawe Phoebe.

So lost was she in her own imaginations, that she neither heard Madam ring her little hand-bell, nor was conscious that the horses had trotted past the window, until Sukey, one of Madam's maids, came in answer to the bell, and courtesying, said, "An it please you, Madam, Mrs Phoebe Latrobe."

Rhoda lifted her eyes eagerly, and saw her cousin. The first item which she noticed was that Phoebe's figure was by no means so good as her own, her shoulders being so high as almost to reach deformity; the next point was that the expression of Phoebe's face was remarkably sweet; the third was that Phoebe's dress was particularly shabby. It was a brown stuff, worn threadbare, too short for the fashion, and without any of the flounces and furbelows then common. Over it was tied a plain white linen apron—aprons were then worn both in and out of doors—and Phoebe's walking costume consisted of a worn black mantua or pelisse, and a hood, brown like the dress, which was the shabbiest of all. The manner of the wearer, however, while extremely modest and void of self-assertion, was not at all awkward nor disconcerted. She courtesied, first to her grandmother, then to her cousin, and stood waiting within the door till she was called forward.

"Come hither, child!" said Madam.

Phoebe walked forward to her, and dropped another courtesy. Madam put two fingers under Phoebe's chin, and lifting up the young face, studied it intently. What she saw there seemed to please her.

"You'll do, child," she said, letting Phoebe go. "Be a good maid, and obedient, and you shall find me your friend. Sit down, and loose your hood. Rhode, pour her a dish of tea."

And this was Madam's welcome to her granddaughter.

Phoebe obeyed her instructions with no words but "Thank you, Madam." Her voice was gentle and low. If the tears burned under her eyelids, no one knew it but herself.

"Take Phoebe upstairs, Rhoda, to your chamber," said Madam, when the new-comer had finished her tea. "I see, child, your new clothes had better not be long a-coming."

"I have a better gown than this, Madam, in my trunk," she answered.

"Well, I am glad of it," said Madam shortly.

Rhoda led her cousin up the wide stone staircase, and into a pretty room, low but comfortable, fitted with a large bed, a washstand, a wardrobe, and a dressing-table. The two girls were to occupy it together. And here Rhoda's tongue, always restrained in her grandmother's presence, felt itself at liberty, and behaved accordingly. A new cousin to catechise was a happiness that did not occur every day.

Emily Sarah Holt

"Have you no black gown?" was the first thing which Rhoda demanded of Phoebe.

"Oh, yes," said Phoebe. "I wear black for my father, and all of them."

Heedless of what she might have noticed—the tremor of Phoebe's voice—Rhoda went on with her catechism.

"How long has your father been dead?"

"Eight months."

"Did you like him?"

"*Like* him!" Phoebe seemed to have no words to answer.

"I never knew anything about mine," went on Rhoda. "He lived till I was thirteen; and I never saw him. Only think!"

Phoebe gave a little shake of her head, as if *her* thoughts were too much for her.

"And my mother died when I was a week old; and I never had any brother or sister," pursued Rhoda.

"Then you never had any one to love? Poor Cousin!" said Phoebe, looking at Rhoda with deep compassion.

"Love! Oh, I don't know that I want it," said Rhoda lightly. "How is Aunt Anne, and where is she?"

"Mother?" Phoebe's voice shook again. "She is going to live with a gentlewoman at the Bath. She stayed till I was gone."

"Well, you know," was the next remark of Rhoda, whose

ideas were not at all neatly put in order, "you'll have to wear a black gown to-morrow. It is King Charles."

"Yes, I know," said Phoebe.

"Was your father a Dissenter?" queried Rhoda.

"No," said Phoebe, looking rather surprised.

"Because I can tell you, Madam hates Dissenters," said Rhoda. "She would as soon have a crocodile to dinner. Why didn't you come in your black gown?"

"It is my best," answered Phoebe. "I cannot afford to spoil it."

"What do you think of Madam?"

Phoebe shrank from this question. "I can hardly think anything yet."

"Oh dear, I wish to-morrow were over!" said Rhoda with an artificial shiver. "I do hate the thirtieth of January. I wish it never came. We have to go to church, and there is only tea and bread and butter for dinner, and we must not divert ourselves with anything. I'll show you the ruins, and read you some of my poetry. Did you not know I writ poetry?"

"No," replied Phoebe. "But will that not be diverting ourselves?"

"Oh, but we can't always be miserable!" said Rhoda. "Besides, what good does it do? It is none to King Charles: and I'm sure it never does me good. Oh, and we will go and see the Maidens' Lodge, and make acquaintance with the old gentlewomen."

Emily Sarah Holt

"The Maidens' Lodge, what is that?"

"Why, about ten years ago Madam built six little houses, and called it the Maidens' Lodge; a sort of better-most kind of alms-houses, you know, for six old gentlewomen—at least, I dare say they are not all old, but some of them are. (Mrs Vane does not think she is, at any rate.) You can't see them from this window; they are on the other side of the church."

"And are they all filled?"

"All but one, just now. I protest I don't know why Madam built them. I guess she thought it was good works. I should have thought it would have been better works to have sent for Aunt Anne, as well as you; but don't you tell her I said so!"

"Don't be afraid," said Phoebe, smiling. "I trust I am not a pick-thank. But don't you think, when you would not have a thing said again, it were better not to say it at the first?"

[Note: A meddlesome mischief-maker.]

"Oh, stuff! I can't always be such a prig as that!"

Phoebe was unpacking a trunk of very modest dimensions, and Rhoda, perched on a corner of the bed, sat and watched her.

"Is *that* your best gown?"

"Yes," said Phoebe, lifting it carefully out.

"How many have you?"

"This and that."

"Only two? How poor Aunt Anne must be!"

"We have always been poor."

"Have you always lived in Bristol?"

"No. We used to live at the Bath when I was a child. Father was curate at the Abbey Church."

"How much did he get?"

"Twenty-five pounds a year."

"That wasn't much for seven of you."

"It was not," returned Phoebe, significantly.

"What can you do?" asked Rhoda, suddenly. "Can you write poetry?"

"I never tried, so I cannot tell," said Phoebe.

"Can you sing?"

"Yes."

"And play on anything?"

"No. I cannot do much. I can sew pretty well, and knit in four different ways; I don't cook much—I mean, I don't know how to make many things, but I always try to be nice in all I can do. I can read and write, and keep accounts."

"Can you dance a jig?—and embroider, and work tapestry?"

"No, I don't know anything of that."

"Can't work tapestry! Why, Phoebe!"

"You see, there never was any time," said Phoebe, apologetically. "Of course, I helped mother with the cooking and sewing; and then there were the children to see to, and I learned Perry and Kitty to read and sew. Then there were all the salves and physic for the poor folk. We could not afford much in that way, but we did what we could."

"Well, I wouldn't marry a parson; that's flat!" said Rhoda. "Fancy spending all your days a-making salves and boluses! Fiddle-faddle!"

Phoebe gave a little laugh. "I was not always making salves," she said.

"Had you any pets? We have a parrot; I believe she's near as old as Madam. I want a monkey, but Madam won't hear of it."

"We never had but one," said Phoebe, the quiver coming again into her voice, "and—it died."

"What was it?"

"A little dog."

"I don't much care for dogs," said Rhoda. "Mrs Vane is the one for pets; that is, whenever they are modish. She carries dormice in her pocket, and keeps a lapdog and a squirrel. When the mode goes out, she gives the thing away, and gets something newer."

"Oh, dear!" said Phoebe. "I could never give my friends away."

"Oh, it is not always to friends," said Rhoda, misunderstanding her. "She gave one of her cats to a tailor at Tewkesbury."

"But the creatures are your friends," said Phoebe. "How can you bear to give them away?"

"Cats, and dogs, and squirrels—friends!" answered Rhoda, laughing. "Why, Phoebe, what a droll creature you are!"

"They would be my friends," responded Phoebe.

"I vow, I'd like to see you make a friend of Mrs Vane's Cupid!" exclaimed Rhoda, laughing. "He is the most spiteful little brute I ever set eyes on. He thinks his teeth were made to bite everybody, and his tail wasn't made to wag."

"Poor little thing! I don't wonder, if he has a mistress who would give him away because it was not the mode to keep him."

"I never saw a maid so droll!" said Rhoda, still laughing; "'twill never serve to be so mighty nice, that I can tell you. Why, you talk as if those creatures had feelings, like we have!"

"And so they have," said Phoebe, warming up a little.

"You are mightily mistaken," returned Rhoda.

"Why do they bark, and bite, and wag their tails, then?" said Phoebe, unanswerably. "It means something."

"Why, what does it signify if they have?" demanded Rhoda, not very consistently. "I say, Phoebe, is that your best hood? How shabby you go!"

Emily Sarah Holt

"Yes," answered Phoebe, quietly.

"How much pin-money do you mean to stand for?" was Rhoda's next startling question.

"How much what?" said astonished Phoebe, dropping the gloves she was taking out of her trunk.

"How much pin-money will you make your husband give you?"

"I've not got one!" was Phoebe's very innocent response.

"Well, you'll have one some day, of course," said Rhoda. "I mean to have five hundred, at least."

"Pounds?" gasped Phoebe.

"Of course!" laughed Rhoda. "I tell you, I mean to be a modish gentlewoman, as good as ever Mrs Vane; and I'll have a knight at least. Oh, you'll see, one of these days. I can manage Madam, when I determine on it. Phoebe, there's the supper bell. Come on."

And quite regardless of the treasonable language in which she had just been indulging, Rhoda danced down into the parlour, becoming suddenly sober as she crossed the threshold.

Phoebe followed, and unless her face much belied her thoughts, she was a good deal puzzled by her new cousin.

CHAPTER TWO

MAKING ACQUAINTANCES

"Ah, be not sad, although thy lot be cast Far from the flock, and in a distant waste: No shepherds' tents within thy view appear, Yet the Chief Shepherd is for ever near."

Cowper.

The Abbey Church of White-Ladies, to which allusion has already been made, was not in any condition for Divine Service, being only a beautiful ruin. When Madam went to church, therefore, she drove two miles to Tewkesbury.

At nine o'clock punctually, the great lumbering coach was drawn to the door by the two heavy Flanders mares, with long black tails which almost touched the ground. Madam, in a superb costume of black satin, trimmed with dark fur and white lace, took her seat in the place of honour. Rhoda, in a satin gown and hood, with a silk petticoat, all black, as became the day, sat on the small seat at one side of the door. But Rhoda sat with her face to the horses, while the yet lower place opposite was reserved for Phoebe, in her unpretending mourning. The great coach rumbled off, out of the grand gates, always opened when Madam was present, past the ruins of the Abbey Church, and drew up before a

Emily Sarah Holt

row of six little houses, fronted by six little gardens. They were built on a very minute scale, exactly alike, each containing four small rooms—kitchen, parlour, and two bedrooms over, with a little lean-to scullery at the back. On the mid-most coping-stone appeared a lofty inscription to the effect that—

"The Maidens' Lodge was built to the Praise and Glory of God, by the pious care of Mistress Perpetua Furnival, Widow, for the lodging of six decayed gentlewomen, Spinsters, of Good Birth and Quality,—A.D. 1702."

It occurred to Phoebe, as she sat reading the inscription, that it might have been pleasanter to the decayed gentlewomen in question not to have their indigence quite so openly proclaimed to the world, even though coupled with good birth and quality, and redounding to the fame of Mistress Perpetua Furnival. But Phoebe had not much time to meditate; for the door of the first little house opened, and down the gravel walk, towards the carriage, came the neatest and nicest of little old ladies, attired, like everybody that day, in black, and carrying a silver-headed cane, on which she leaned as if it really were needed to support her. She was one of those rare persons, a pretty old woman. Her complexion was still as fair and delicate as a painting on china, her blue eyes clear and expressive. Of course, in days when everyone wore powder, hair was of one colour—white.

"This is Mrs Dolly Jennings," whispered Rhoda to Phoebe; "she is the eldest of the maidens, and she is about seventy. I believe she is some manner of cousin to the Duke—not very near, you know."

The Duke, in 1712, of course, meant the Duke of Marlborough.

"Good morning, Madam," said Mrs Jennings, in a cheerful yet gentle voice, when she reached the carriage.

"Good morning, Mrs Dorothy. I am glad I see you well enough to accompany me to church."

"You are very good, Madam," was the reply, as Mrs Dorothy clambered up into the lumbering vehicle; "I thank God my rheumatic pains are as few and easy to-day as an old woman of threescore and ten need look for."

"You are a great age, Mrs Dorothy," observed Madam.

"Yes, Madam, I thank God," returned Mrs Dorothy, as cheerfully as before.

While Phoebe was meditating on this last answer, the second Maiden appeared from Number Two. She was an entire contrast to the first, being tall, sharp, featured, florid, high-nosed, and generally angular.

"Mrs Jane Talbot," whispered Rhoda.

Mrs Jane, having offered her civilities to Madam, climbed also into the coach, and placed herself beside Mrs Dorothy.

"Marcella begs you will allow her excuses, Madam, for she is indisposed this morning," said Mrs Jane, in a quick, sharp voice, which made Phoebe doubt if all her angularity were outside.

While Madam was expressing her regret at this news, the doors of Numbers Five and Six opened simultaneously, and two ladies emerged, who were, in their way, as much a contrast as Mrs Jane and Mrs Dorothy. Number Six reached the carriage first. She was a pleasant, comfortable looking woman of about fifty years of age, with a round face and healthy complexion, and a manner which, while kindly, was dignified and self-possessed.

"Good morning, my Lady Betty!" said the three voices.

Phoebe then perceived that the seat of honour, beside Madam, had been reserved for Lady Betty. But Number Five followed, and she was so singular a figure that Phoebe's attention was at once diverted to her.

She looked about the age of Lady Betty, but having evidently been a beauty in her younger days she was greatly indisposed to resign that character. Though it was a sharp January morning, her neck was unprotected by the warm tippet which all the other ladies wore. There was nothing to keep her warm in that quarter except a necklace. Large ear-rings depended from her ears, half a dozen rings were worn outside her gloves, a long chatelaine hung from her neck to her waist, to which were attached a bunch of trinkets of all shapes and sizes. She was laced very tight, and her poor nose was conscious of it, as it showed by blushing at the enormity. Under her left arm was a very small, very fat, very blunt-nosed Dutch pug. Phoebe at once guessed that the lady was Mrs Vane, and that the pug was Cupid.

"Well, Clarissa!" said Mrs Jane, as the new-comer took her seat at the door opposite Rhoda; "pity you hadn't a nose-ring!"

Mrs Vane made no answer beyond an affected smile, but Cupid growled at Mrs Jane, whom he did not seem to hold in high esteem. The coach, with a good effort on the part of the horses, got under way, and rumbled off towards Tewkesbury.

"And how does Sir Richard, my Lady Betty?" inquired

Madam, with much cordiality.

"Oh, extremely well, I thank you," answered Lady Betty. "So well, indeed, now, that he talks of a journey to London, and a month at the Bath on his way thence."

"What takes him to London?" asked Mrs Jane.

"'Tis for the maids he thinks to go. He would have Betty and Gatty have a season's polishing; and for Molly—poor little soul!—he is wishful to have her touched."

"Is she as ill for the evil as ever, poor child?"

"Oh, indeed, yes! 'Tis a thousand pities; and such sprightly parts as she discovers!"

[Note: So clever as she is.]

"'Tis a mercy for such as she that the Queen doth touch," said Mrs Jane. "King William never did."

"Is that no mistake?" gently suggested Lady Betty.

"Never *dared*," came rather grimly from Madam.

"Well, maybe," said Mrs Jane. "But I protest I cannot see why Queen Mary should not have done it, as well as her sister."

"I own I cannot but very much doubt," returned Madam, severely, "that any good consequence should follow."

By which it will be perceived that Madam was an uncompromising Jacobite. Mrs Jane had no particular convictions, but she liked to talk Whig, because all around were Tories. Lady

Betty was a Hanoverian Tory—that is, what would be termed an extreme Tory in the present day, but attached to the Protestant Succession. Mrs Clarissa was whatever she found it the fashion to be. As to Mrs Dorothy, she held private opinions, but she never allowed them to appear, well knowing that they would be far from acceptable to Madam. And since Mrs Dorothy was sometimes constrained unwillingly to differ from Madam on points which she deemed essential, she was careful not to vex her on subjects which she considered indifferent.

Rhoda was rather disappointed to find that Phoebe showed no astonished admiration of Tewkesbury Abbey. She forgot that the Abbey Church at Bath, and Saint Mary Redcliffe at Bristol, had been familiar to Phoebe from her infancy. The porch was lined with beggars, who showered blessings upon Madam, in grateful anticipation of shillings to come. But Madam passed grandly on, and paid no attention to them.

The church and the service were about equally chilly. Being a fast-day, the organ was silent; but all the responding was left to the choir, the congregation seemingly supposing it as little their concern as Cupid thought it his—who curled himself up comfortably, and went to sleep. The gentlemen appeared to be amusing themselves by staring at the ladies; the ladies either returned the compliment slily behind their fans, or exchanged courtesies with each other. There was a long, long bidding prayer, and a sermon which might have been fitly prefaced by the announcement, "Let us talk to the praise and glory of Charles the First!" It was over at last. The gentlemen put down their eye-glasses, the ladies yawned and furled their fans; there was a great deal of bowing, and courtesying, and complimenting—Mr William informing Mrs Betty that the sun had come out solely to do her honour, and Mrs Betty retorting with a delicate blow from her fan, and, "What a mad fellow are you!" At last these also were over; and the ladies from Cressingham remounted the family coach, nearly in the same order as they came—the variation being that Phoebe found herself seated opposite Mrs Clarissa Vane.

"Might I pat him?" said Phoebe, diffidently.

"If you want to be bit, do!" snapped Mrs Jane.

"Oh deah, yes!" languishingly responded Mrs Clarissa. "He neveh bites, does 'e, the pwetty deah!"

"Heyday! Doesn't 'e, the pwetty deah!" observed Mrs Jane, in such exact imitation of her friend's affected tones as sorely to try Phoebe's gravity.

Lady Betty laughed openly, but added, "Mind what you are about, child."

"Poor doggie!" softly said Phoebe.

Cupid's response was the slightest oscillation of the extreme point of his tail. But when Phoebe attempted to stroke him, to the surprise of all parties, instead of snapping at her, as he was expected to do, Cupid only wagged rather more decidedly; and when Phoebe proceeded to rub his head and ears, he actually gave her, not a bite of resentment, but a lick of friendliness.

"Deah! the sweet little deah! 'E's vewy good!" said his mistress.

The gentle reader is requested not to suppose that the elision of Mrs Clarissa's poor letter H, as well as R, proceeded either from ignorance or vulgarity—except so far as vulgarity lies in blindly following fashion. Mrs Clarissa's only mistake was that, like most country ladies, she was rather behind the age. The dropping of H and other letters had been fashionable in the metropolis some eight years before.

"Clarissa, what a goose are you!" said Mrs Jane.

"Come, Jenny, don't you bite!" put in Lady Betty. "Cupid has set you a better example than so."

"I'll not bite Clarissa, I thank you," was Mrs Jane's rather spiteful answer. "It would want more than one fast-day to bring me to that. Couldn't fancy the paint. And don't think I could digest the patches."

Lady Betty appeared to enjoy Mrs Jane's very uncivil speeches; while Cupid's mistress remained untouched by them, being one of those persons who affect not to hear anything to which they do not choose to respond.

"Well, Rhoda, child," said Lady Betty, as the coach neared home, "'tis no good, I guess, to bid you drink tea on a fast-day?"

"Oh, but I am coming, my Lady Betty," answered Rhoda, briskly. "I mean to drink a dish with every one of you."

"I shan't give you anything to eat," interpolated Mrs Jane. "Never do to be guzzling on a fast-day. You won't get any sugar from me, neither."

"Never mind, Mrs Jane," said Rhoda. "Mrs Dolly will give me something, I know. And I shall visit her first."

Mrs Dorothy assented by a benevolent smile.

"I hope, child, you will not forget it is a fast-day," said

Madam, gravely, "and not go about to divert yourself in an improper manner."

"Oh no, Madam!" said Rhoda, drawing in her horns.

No sooner was dinner over—and as Rhoda had predicted, there was nothing except boiled potatoes and bread and butter—than Rhoda pounced on Phoebe, and somewhat authoritatively bade her come upstairs. Madam had composed herself in her easy chair, with the "Eikon Basilike" in her hand.

"Will Madam not be lonely?" asked Phoebe, timidly, as she followed Rhoda.

"Lonely? Oh, no! She'll be asleep in a minute," said Rhoda.

"I thought she was going to read," suggested Phoebe.

"She fancies so," said Rhoda, laughing. "I never knew her try yet but she went to sleep directly."

Unlocking a closet door which stood in their bedroom, and climbing on a chair to reach the top shelf, Rhoda produced a small volume bound in red sheepskin, which she introduced to Phoebe's notice with a rather grandiloquent air.

"Now, Phoebe! There's my Book of Poems!"

Phoebe opened the book, and her eye fell on a few lines of faint, delicate writing, on the fly-leaf.

"To Rhoda Peveril, with her Aunt Margaret's love."

"Oh, you have an aunt!" said Phoebe.

"I have two somewhere," said Rhoda. "They are good for nothing. They never give me anything."

Phoebe looked up with a rather surprised air. "They seem to do, sometimes," she observed, pointing to the book.

"Well, that one did," answered Rhoda; "one or two little things like that; but she is dead. The others are just a pair of spiteful old cats."

Phoebe's look of astonishment deepened.

"They must be very different from my aunt, then. I have only one, but I would not call her names for the world. She loves me, and I love her."

"Why, what are aunts good for but to be called names?" was the amiable response. "But now listen, Phoebe. I am going to read you a piece of my poetry. You see, our old church is dedicated to Saint Ursula; and there is an image in the church, which they say is Saint Ursula—it has such a charming face! Madam doesn't think 'tis charming, but I do. So you see, this poem is to that image."

Phoebe looked rather puzzled, but did not answer.

"Now, I would have you criticise, Phoebe," said Rhoda, condescendingly, using a word she had picked up from one of her grandfather's books.

"I don't know what that is," said Phoebe.

"Well, it means, if you hear anything you don't like, say so."

"Very well," replied Phoebe, quietly.

And Rhoda began to read, with the style of a rhetorician—as she supposed—

"Step softly, nearer as ye tread
To this shrine of the royal dead!
This Abbey's hallowed unto one,
Daughter of Britain's ancient throne,—
History names her one sole thing,
The daughter of a British King."

Rhoda paused, and looked at her cousin—ostensibly for criticism, really for admiration. If Phoebe had said exactly what she thought, it would have been that her ear was cruelly outraged: but Phoebe was not accustomed to the sharp speeches which passed for wit with Rhoda. She fell back on a matter of fact.

"Does history say nothing more about her?"

"Of course it does! It says the Vandals martyred her. Phoebe, you can't criticise poetry as if it were prose."

It struck Phoebe that Rhoda's poetry was very like prose; but she said meekly, "Please go on. I ask your pardon."

So Rhoda went on—

"Her glorious line has passed away—
The wild dream of a by-gone day!
We know not from what throne she sprang,
Britain is silent in her song—"

"What's the matter?" asked Rhoda, interrupting herself.

"I ask your pardon," said Phoebe again. "But—will *song* do with *sprang*? And if Ursula was a real person, as I thought she had been, she wasn't a wild dream, was she?"

"Phoebe, I do believe you haven't a bit of taste!" said Rhoda. "I'll try you with one more verse, and then—

"O wake her not! Ages have passed
Since her fair eyelids closed at last."

"I should think, then, you would find it difficult to wake her," remarked Phoebe: but Rhoda went on as if she had not heard it,—

"For twice six hundred years, 'tis said,
Hath rested 'neath yon tomb her head,—
That head which soft reposed of old
On couch of satin and of gold."

"Dear!" was Phoebe's comment. "I didn't know they had satin sofas twelve hundred years ago."

"'Tis no earthly use reading poetry to you!" exclaimed Rhoda, throwing down the book. "You haven't one bit of feeling for it, no more than if it were a sermon I was reading! Tie your hood on, and make haste, and we'll go and see the Maidens."

Phoebe seemed rather troubled to have annoyed her cousin, though she evidently did not perceive how it had been effected. The girls tied on their hoods, and Rhoda, who was not really ill-natured, soon recovered herself when she got into the fresh air.

"Now, while we are going across the Park," she said, "I will tell you something about the old gentlewomen. I couldn't this morning, you know, more than their names, because there was Madam listening. But now, hark! Mrs Dolly Jennings—

the one who came in first, you know, and sat over against Lady Betty—I don't know what kin she is, but there is some kin between her and the Duchess of Marlborough. She is the oldest of the Maidens, and the best one to tell a story—except she falls to preaching, and then 'tis tiresome. Do you like sermons, Phoebe?"

"It all depends who preaches them," said Phoebe.

"Well, of course it does," said Rhoda. "I don't like anyone but Dr Harris—he has such white hands!"

"He does not preach about them, does he?" said Phoebe, apparently puzzled as to the connection.

"Oh, he nourishes them about, and discovers so many elegancies!" answered Rhoda.

"But how does that make him preach better?"

"Why, Phoebe, how stupid you are! But you must not interrupt me in that way, or I shall never be done. Mrs Dolly, you see, is seventy or more; and in her youth she was in the great world. So she has all manner of stories, and she'll always tell them when you ask her. I only wish she did not preach! Well, then, Mrs Jane Talbot—that one with the high nose, that sat next Mrs Dolly in the coach—she has lively parts enough, and that turn makes her very agreeable. I don't care for her sister, Mrs Marcella, that lives next her—she's always having some distemper, and I don't like sick people. Mrs Clarissa Vane is the least well-born of all of them; but she's been a toast, you see, and she fancies herself charming, poor old thing! As for Lady Betty—weren't you surprised? I believe Madam pays her a good lot to live there; it gives the place an air, you know. She is Sir Richard Delawarr's aunt, and he is the great man all about here—all the land that way belongs to him, as far as you can see. He is of very good family—an old Norman house. They are thought a great deal of, you know."

"But isn't that strange?" said Phoebe, meditatively. "If Sir Richard is thought more of because his forefathers came from France six hundred years ago, why is my grandfather thought less of because he came from France thirty years ago?"

"O Phoebe! It is not the same thing at all!"

"But why is it not the same thing?" gently persisted Phoebe.

"Oh, nonsense!" said Rhoda, cutting the knot peremptorily. "Phoebe, can you speak French?"

"Yes."

"Have a care you don't let Madam hear you! Who taught you?—your father?"

"Yes. He said it was our own language."

"Why, you don't mean to say he was *proud* of being a Frenchman?" cried Rhoda, in amazement.

"I think he was, if he was proud of anything," answered Phoebe. "He loved France very dearly. He thought it the grandest country in the world."

And Phoebe's voice trembled a little. Evidently her father was in her eyes a hero, and all that he had loved was sacred.

"But, Phoebe! not greater than England? He couldn't!" cried Rhoda, to whom such an idea seemed an impossibility.

"He was fond of England, too," said Phoebe. "He said she had sheltered us when our own country cast us off, and we should love her and be very thankful to her. But he loved France the best."

Rhoda tried to accept this incredible proposition.

"Well! 'tis queer!" she said at last. "Proud of being a Frenchman! What would Madam say?"

"'Tis only like Sir Richard Delawarr, is it?"

"Phoebe, you've no sense!"

"Well, perhaps I haven't," said Phoebe meekly, as they turned in at the gate of Number One.

Mrs Dolly Jennings was ready for her guests, in her little parlour, with the most delicate and transparent china set out upon the little tea-table, and the smallest and brightest of copper kettles singing on the hob.

"Well, you thought I meant it, Mrs Dolly!" exclaimed Rhoda laughingly, as the girls entered.

"I always think people mean what they say, child, until I find they don't," said Mrs Dorothy. "Welcome, Miss Phoebe, my dear!"

"Oh, would you please to call me Phoebe?" said the owner of that name, blushing.

"So I will, my dear," replied Mrs Dorothy, who was busy now pouring out the tea. "Mrs Rhoda, take a chair, child, and help yourself to bread and butter."

Emily Sarah Holt

Rhoda obeyed, and did not pass the plate to Phoebe.

"Mrs Dolly," she said, interspersing her words with occasional bites, "I am really concerned about Phoebe. She hasn't the least bit of sense."

"Indeed, child," quietly responded Mrs Dorothy, while Phoebe coloured painfully. "How doth she show it?"

"Why, she doesn't care a straw for poetry?"

"Is it poetry you engaged her with?"

"What do you mean?" said Rhoda, rather pettishly. "It was my poetry."

"Eh, dear!" said Mrs Dorothy, but there was a little indication of fun about her mouth. "Perhaps, my dear, you write lyrics, and your cousin hath more fancy for epical poetry."

"She doesn't care for any sort, I'm sure," said Rhoda.

"What say you to this heavy charge, Phoebe?" inquired little Mrs Dorothy, with a cheery smile.

"I like some poetry," replied Phoebe, bashfully.

"What kind?" blurted out Rhoda, apparently rather affronted.

Phoebe coloured, and hesitated. "I like the old hymns the Huguenots used to sing," she said, "such us dear father taught me."

"Hymns aren't poetry!" said Rhoda, contemptuously.

"That is true enough of some hymns, child," answered Mrs

Dorothy. "But, Phoebe, my dear, will you let us hear one of your hymns?"

"They are in French," whispered Phoebe.

"They will do for me in French, my dear," replied Mrs Dorothy.

Rhoda stared in manifest astonishment. Phoebe struggled for a moment with her natural shyness, and then she began:—

"Mon sort n'est pas a plaindre,
Il est a desirer;
Je n'ai plus rien a craindre,
Car Dieu est mon Berger."

"My lot asks no complaining,
But joy and confidence;
I have no fear remaining,
For God is my Defence."

But the familiar words evidently brought with them a rush of associations which was too much for Phoebe. She burst in tears, and covered her face with her hands.

"What on earth are you crying for?" asked Rhoda.

"Thank you, my dear," said Mrs Dorothy. "The verse is enough for a day, and the truth which is in it is enough for a life."

"I ask your pardon!" sobbed Phoebe, when she could speak at all. "But I used to sing it—to dear father, and when he was gone I said it to poor mother. And they are all gone now!"

"Oh, don't bother!" said Rhoda. "My papa's dead, and my

Emily Sarah Holt

mamma too; but you'll not see me crying over it."

Rhoda pronounced the words "Pappa," and "Mamma," as is done in America to this day.

"You never knew your parents, Mrs Rhoda," said the little old lady, ever ready to cast oil on the troubled waters. "Phoebe, dear child, wouldst thou wish them all back again?"

"No; oh, no! I could not be so unkind," said Phoebe, wiping her eyes. "But only a year ago, there were seven of us. It seems so hard!"

"I say, Phoebe, if you mean to cry and take on," said Rhoda, springing up and drinking off her tea, "you'll give me the spleen. I hate to be hipped. I shall be off to Mrs Jane. Come along!"

"Go yourself, Mrs Rhoda, my dear, and leave your cousin to recover, if tears be your aversion."

"Why, aren't they all our aversions?" said Rhoda, outraging grammar. "You don't need to pretend, Mrs Dolly! I never saw you cry in my life."

"Ah, child!" said Mrs Dorothy, as if she meant to indicate that there had been more of her life than could be seen from Rhoda's standing-point. "But you'll do well to take an old woman's counsel, my dear. Run off to Mrs Jane, and divert yourself half an hour; and when you return, your cousin will have passed her trouble, and I will have a Story to tell you both. I know you like stories."

"Come, I'll go, for a story when I came back," said Rhoda; "but I meant to take Phoebe. Can't she wipe her eyes and come?"

"Then I shall not tell you a story," responded Mrs Dorothy.

Rhoda laughed, and ran off. Mrs Dorothy let Phoebe have her cry out for a short time. She moved softly about, putting things in order, and then came and sat down by Phoebe on the settle.

"The world is too great for thee, poor child!" she said, tenderly, taking Phoebe's hands in hers. "It is a long way from thy father's grave; but, bethink thee, 'tis no long way from himself, if he is gone to Him that is our Father."

"I know he is," whispered Phoebe.

"And is the Lord thy Shepherd, dear child?"

"I know He is," said Phoebe, again.

"'Mon sort n'est pas a plaindre,'" softly repeated Mrs Dorothy.

"Oh, it is wrong of me!" sobbed Phoebe. "But it does seem so hard. Nobody cares for me any more."

"Nay, my child, 'He careth for thee.'"

"Oh, I know it is so!" was the answer; "but I can't feel it. It all looks so dark and cold. I can't feel it!"

"Poor little child, lost in the dark!" said Mrs Dorothy, gently. "Dear, the Lord must know how very much easier it would be to see. But His especial blessing is spoken on them that have not seen, and yet have believed. 'Tis an honour to thy Father, little Phoebe, to put thine hand in His, and let

Emily Sarah Holt

Him lead thee where He will. Thine earthly father would have liked thee to trust him. Canst thou not trust the heavenly Father?"

Phoebe's tears were falling more softly now.

"Phoebe, little maiden, shall I love thee?"

"Thank you, Mrs Dorothy, but people don't love me," said Phoebe, as if it were a fact, sad, indeed, but incontrovertible. "Only dear father and Perry."

"And thy mother," suggested Mrs Dorothy, in a soothing tone.

"Well—yes—I suppose so," doubtfully admitted Phoebe. "But, you see, poor mother—I had better not talk about it, Mrs Dorothy, if you please."

Mrs Dorothy let the point pass, making a note of it in her own mind. She noticed, too, that Phoebe said, "Dear father" and "poor mother"; yet it was the father who was dead, and the mother was living. The terms, thought Mrs Dorothy, must have some reference to character.

"Little Phoebe," she said, "if it should comfort thee betimes to pour out thine heart to some human creature, come across the Park, and tell thy troubles to me. Thou art but a young traveller; and such mostly long for some company. Yet, bethink thee, my dear, I can but be sorry for thee, while the Lord can help thee. He is the best to trust, child."

"Yes, I know," whispered Phoebe. "You are so good, Mrs Dorothy!"

"Now for the story!" said Rhoda, dancing into the little

parlour. "You've had oceans of time to dry your eyes. I have been to Mrs Jane, and Mrs Clarissa, and my Lady Betty; and I've had a dish of tea with each one. I shall turn into a tea-plant presently. Now I'm ready, Mrs Dorothy; go on!"

"What fashion of tale should you like, Mrs Rhoda?"

"Oh, you had better begin at the beginning," said Rhoda. "I don't think I ever heard you tell about when you were a child; you always begin with the Revolution. Go back a little earlier, and let us have your whole history."

Mrs Dorothy paused thoughtfully.

"It won't do me any harm," added Rhoda; "and I can't see why you should care. You're nearly seventy, aren't you?"

Phoebe's shy glance at her cousin might have been inter-preted to mean that she did not think her very civil; but Mrs Dorothy did not resent the question.

"Yes, my dear, I am over seventy," she said, quietly. "And I don't know that it would do you any harm. You have to face the world, too, one of these days. Please God, you may have a more guarded entrance into it than I had! Here is a cushion for your back, Mrs Rhoda; and, Phoebe, my dear, here is one for you. Let me reach my knitting, and then you shall hear my story. But it will be a long one."

"So much the better, if 'tis agreeable," answered Rhoda. "I don't care for stories that are over in a minute."

"This will not be over in a day," said Mrs Dorothy.

"All right," responded Rhoda, settling herself as comfortably

Emily Sarah Holt

as she could. "I say, Phoebe, change cushions with me; I'm sure you've got the softer."

And Phoebe obeyed in an instant.

CHAPTER THREE

LITTLE MRS. DOROTHY

"And the thousands come and go
All along the crowded street;
But they give no ear to the things we know,
And they pass with careless feet.
For some hearts are hard with gold,
And some are crushed in the throng,
And some with the pleasures of life are cold—
How long, O Lord, how long!"

"If I am to begin at the beginning, my dears," said little Mrs Dorothy, "I must tell you that I was born in a farmhouse, about a mile from Saint Albans, on the last day of the year of our Lord 1641; that my father was the Reverend William Jennings, brother to Sir Edward; and that my mother was Mrs Frances, daughter to Sir Jeremy Charlton."

"Whatever made your father take up with a parson's life?" said Rhoda. "I wouldn't be one for an apron full of money! Surely he was married first, wasn't he?"

"He was married first," answered Mrs Dorothy; "and both his father and my mother's kindred took it extreme ill that he should propose such views to himself,—the rather because

　　　　　Emily Sarah Holt

he was of an easy fortune, his grandmother having left him some money."

"Would I have been a parson!" exclaimed Rhoda. "I'm too fond of jellies and conserves—nobody better."

"Well, my dear Mrs Rhoda, if you will have me say what I think," resumed Mrs Dorothy.

"You can if you like," interjected Rhoda.

"It does seem to me, and hath ever done so, that the common custom amongst us, which will have the chaplain to rise and withdraw when dessert is served, must be a relique of barbarous times."

Dessert at that time included pies, puddings, and jellies.

"O Mrs Dorothy! you have the drollest notions!"

And Rhoda went off in a long peal of laughter. The idea of any other arrangement struck her as very comical indeed.

"Well, my dear," said Mrs Dorothy, "I hope some day to see it otherwise."

"Oh, how droll it would be!" said Rhoda. "But go on, please, Mrs Dolly."

"Through those troublous times that followed on my birth," resumed the old lady, "I was left for better safety with the farmer at whose house I was born; for my father had shortly after been made parson of a church in London, and 'twas not thought well that so young a child as I then was should be bred up in all the city tumults. My foster-father's name was Lawrence Ingham; and he and his good wife were as father and mother to me."

"But what fashion of breeding could you get at a farm-house?" demanded Rhoda, with a scornful pout.

"Why, 'twas not there I learned French, child," answered Mrs Dorothy, smiling; "but I learned to read, write, and cast accounts; to cook and distil, to conserve and pickle; with all manner of handiworks—sewing, knitting, broidery, and such like. And I can tell you, my dear, that in all the great world whereunto I afterwards entered I never saw better manners than in that farmhouse. I saw more ceremonies, sure; but not more courtesy and kindly thought for others."

"Why, I thought folks like that had no manners at all!" said Rhoda.

"Then you were mightily mistaken, my dear. Farmer Ingham had two daughters, who were like sisters to me; but they were both older than I. Their names were Grace and Faith. 'Twas a very quiet, peaceful household. We rose with the sun in summer, and before it in winter—"

"Catch me!" interpolated Rhoda.

"And before any other thing might be done, there was reading and prayer in the farmhouse kitchen. All the farm servants trooped in, and took their places in order, the men on the right hand of the master, and the women on the left of the mistress. Then the farmer read a chapter, and afterwards prayed, all joining in 'Our Father' at the end."

"But—he wasn't a parson?" demanded Rhoda, with a perplexed look.

"Oh no, my dear."

Emily Sarah Holt

"Then how could he pray?" said Rhoda. "He'd no business to read the Prayer-Book; and of course he couldn't pray without it."

"Ah, then he made a mistake," replied Mrs Dorothy very quietly. "He fancied he could."

"But who ever heard of such a thing?" said Rhoda.

"We heard a good deal of it in those days, my dear. Why, child, the Common Prayer was forbid, even in the churches. Nobody used it, save a few here and there, that chose to run the risk of being found out and punished."

"How queer!" cried Rhoda. "Well, go on, Mrs Dolly. I hope the prayers weren't long. I should have wanted my breakfast."

"They were usually about three parts of an hour."

"Ugh!" with a manufactured shudder, came from Rhoda.

"After prayers, for an hour, each went to her calling. Commonly we took it turn about, the girls and I—one with the mistress in the kitchen, one with the maids in the chambers, and the third, if the weather was fine, a-weeding the posies in the garden, or, if wet, at her sewing in the parlour. Then the great bell was rung for breakfast, and we all gathered again in the kitchen. For breakfast were furmety, eggs, and butter, and milk, for the women; cold bakemeats and ale for the men."

"No tea?" asked Rhoda.

"I was near ten years old, child, ere coffee came into England; and tea was some years later. The first coffee-house that ever was in this realm was set up at Oxford, of one Jacobs, a Jew; and about two years after was the first in London. For tea, 'twas said Queen Catherine brought it hither from Portingale; but in truth, I believe 'twas known among us somewhat sooner. But when it came in, for a long time none knew how to use it, except at the coffee-houses. I could tell you a droll tale of a neighbour of Farmer Ingham's, that had a parcel of tea sent her as a great present from London, with a letter that said 'twas all the mode with the quality. And what did she, think you, but boiled it like cabbage, and bade all her neighbours come taste the new greens."

"Did they like them?" asked Rhoda, as well as she could speak for laughing.

"I heard they all thought with their hostess, who said, 'If those were quality greens, the quality were welcome to keep 'em; country folk would rather have cabbage and spinach any day.'"

"Well!" said Rhoda, bridling a little, when her amusement had subsided; "'tis very silly for mean people to ape the quality."

"It is so, my dear," replied Mrs Dorothy, with that extreme quietness which was the nearest her gentle spirit could come to irony. "'Tis silly for any to ape another, be he less or more."

"Why, there can be no communication between them," observed Rhoda, with a toss of her head.

"'Communication,' my dear," said Mrs Dolly. "Yonder's a new word. Where did you pick it up?"

"O Mrs Dolly! you can't be in the mode if you don't pick up

Emily Sarah Holt

all the new words," answered Rhoda more affectedly than ever. She was showing off now, and was entirely in her element.

"And pray what are the other new words, my dear?" inquired Mrs Dorothy good-naturedly, and not without a little amusement. "That one sounds very much like the old-fashioned 'commerce.'"

"Well, I don't know them all!" said Rhoda, with an assumption of humility; "but now-o'-days, when you speak of any one's direction, you must say *adresse*, from the French; and if one is out of spirits, you say he is *hipped*—that's from hypochondriacal; and a crowd of people is a *mob*—that's short for mobile; and when a man goes about, and doesn't want to be known, you say he is *incog.*—that means incognito, which is the Spanish for unknown. Then you say Mr Such-an-one spends *to the tune of five* hundred a year; and there are a lot of men *of his kidney*; and *I bantered them* well about it. Oh, there are lots of new words, Mrs Dolly."

"So it seems, my dear. But are you sure incognito is Spanish?"

"Oh, yes! William Knight told me so," said Rhoda, with another toss of her head.

"I imagined it was Latin," observed Mrs Dorothy. "But 'tis true, I know nought of either tongue."

"Oh, William Knight knows everything," said Rhoda, hyperbolically.

"He must be a very ingenious young man," quietly observed Mrs Dorothy.

"Well, he is," said Rhoda, scarcely perceiving the satire latent in Mrs Dorothy's calm tones.

"I am glad to hear it, my dear," returned the old lady.

"But he's very uppish,—that's pos.," resumed the young one.

"Really, my dear, you are full of new words," said Mrs Dorothy, good-naturedly. "What means 'pos.,' pray you?"

"Why, 'positive,'" said Rhoda, laughing. "And *rep.* means reputation, and *fire* means spirit, and *smart* means sharp, and a *concert* means a lot of people singing and playing on instruments of music, and an *operation* means anything you do, and a *speculation* means—well, it means—it means a speculation, you know."

"Dear, dear!" cried little Mrs Dorothy, holding up her hands. "I protest, my dear, I shall be drove to learn the English tongue anew if this mode go on."

"Well, Mrs Dolly, suppose your tale should go on?" suggested Rhoda. "Heyday! do you know what everybody is saying?—everybody that is anybody, you understand."

"I thought that everybody was somebody," remarked Mrs Dorothy, with a comical set of the lips.

"Oh dear, no!" said Rhoda. "There are ever so many people who are nobody."

"Indeed!" said Mrs Dorothy. "Well, child, what is everybody saying?"

"Why, they say the Duke is not so well with the Queen as he has been. 'Tis thought, I assure you, by many above people."

Emily Sarah Holt

"Is that one of the new words?" inquired Mrs Dorothy, with a little laugh. "Dear child, what mean you?—the angels?"

"Oh, Mrs Dorothy, you are the oddest creature!" cried Rhoda. "Why, you know very well what I mean. Should you be sorry, Mrs Dolly, if the Duke became inconsiderable?"

"No, my dear. Why should I?"

"Well, I thought—" but Rhoda's thought went no further.

"You thought," quietly continued the old lady, "that I had not had enow of town vanities, and would fain climb a few rungs up the ladder, holding on to folks' skirts. Was that it, child?"

"Well, I don't know," said Rhoda uneasily, for Mrs Dorothy had translated her thought into rather too plain language.

"Ah, my dear, that is because you would love to climb a little yourself," said Mrs Dorothy, smilingly, "and you apprehend no inconveniency from it. But, child, 'tis the weariest work in all the world—except it be climbing from earth to heaven. To climb on men's ladders is mostly as a squirrel climbs in its cage,—round and round; you think yourself going vastly higher, but those that stand on the firm ground and watch you see that you do but go round. But to climb up Jacob's ladder, whereof the Lord stands at the top, it will be other eyes that behold you climbing up, when in your own eyes you have not bettered yourself by a step. Climb as high as you will there, dear maids!—but never mind the ladders that go round. They are infinitely disappointing. I know it, for I have climbed them."

"Well, Mrs Dolly, do go on, now, and tell us all about it, there's a good soul!" said Rhoda.

Little Mrs Dorothy was executing some elaborate knitting. She went on with it for a few seconds in silence.

"I was but sixteen," she said, quietly, "when my mother came to visit me. I could not remember seeing her before: and very frighted was I of the grand gentlewoman, for so she seemed to me, that rustled into the farmhouse kitchen in silken brocade, and a velvet tippet on her neck. She was evenly disappointed with me. She thought me stiff and gloomy; and I thought her strange and full of vanities. 'In three years' time, Dolly,' quoth she, 'thou wilt be nineteen, and I will then have thee up to Town, and thou shalt see somewhat of the world. Thou art not ill-favoured,' quoth she,—'twas my mother that said this, my dears," modestly interpolated Mrs Dorothy,—"and I dare say thou wilt be the Town talk in a week. 'Tis pity there is no better world to have thee into!—and thy father as sour and Puritanical as any till of late, save the mark!—but there, 'we must swim with the tide,' saith she. 'Tis a long lane that has no turning.' Ah me! but the lane had turned ere I was nineteen."

"Why, Mrs Dolly, the Restoration must have been that very year," observed Rhoda.

"That very year," repeated Mrs Dorothy. "'Twas in April I quitted Farmer Ingham's house, and was fetched up to London; and in May came the King in, and was shortly thereafter crowned."

"If it please you," asked Phoebe, speaking for the first time of her own accord, "were you glad to go, Madam?"

"Well, my dear, I was partly glad and partly sorry. I was sorrowful to take leave of mine old friends, little knowing if I should ever see them again or no; yet, like an untried maid, I was mightily set up with the thought of seeing London, and the lions, and Whitehall, and the like. Silly maid that I was! I had better have shed tears for the last than for the first."

"What thought you the finest thing in London?" said Rhoda. "But tell us, what thought you of London altogether?"

"Why, the first thing I thought of was the size and the noise," answered Mrs Dorothy. "It seemed to me such a great over-grown town, so different from Saint Albans; and so many carts and wheelbarrows always rattling over the stones; and so many folks in the streets; and all the strange cries of a morning. I thought my father a very strange, cold man, of whom I was no little afraid; and my mother was sadly disappointed that I did not roll my eyes, and had not been taught to dance."

"Why did they ever leave you at a farmhouse?" inquired Rhoda, rather scornfully.

"*I* cannot entirely say, my dear; but I think that was mainly my father's doing. My poor father!"

And Mrs Dorothy's handkerchief was hastily passed across her eyes.

"The first night I came," she said, "my mother had a large assembly in her withdrawing-chamber. There were smart-dressed ladies fluttering of their fans, and gentlemen in all the colours of the rainbow; and I, foolish maid! right well pleased when one and another commended my country complexion, or told me something about my fine eyes: when all at once came a heavy hand on my shoulder, and my father saith, 'Dorothy, I would speak with you.' I followed him forth, not a little trembling lest he should be about to chide me; but he led me into his own closet, and shut the door. He bade me sit, and leaning over the fire himself, he said nought for a moment. Then saith he, 'Dorothy, you heard Mr Debenham speak to you?' 'Yes, Sir,' quoth I. 'And what said he, child?' goes on my father, gently. I was something loth to repeat what he had said; for it was what I, in my foolish heart, thought a very fine speech about Mrs Doll's fine eyes, that glistered like stars. Howbeit, my father waited quiet enough; and having been well bred to obey by Farmer Ingham, I brought it out at last. 'Did you believe it, Dorothy?' saith my father. 'Did you think he meant it?' I did but whisper, 'Yes, Sir,' for I could not but feel very much ashamed. 'Then, Dorothy,' saith he, 'the first lesson you will do well to learn in London is that men and women do not always mean it when they flatter you. And he does not. Ah!' saith my father, fetching a great sigh,—"tis easy work for fathers to say such things, but not so for maidens to believe them. There is one other thing I would have you learn, Dorothy.' 'Yes, Sir,' quoth I, when he stayed. He turned him around, and looked in my face with his dark eyes, that seemed to burn into me, and he saith, 'Learn this, Dorothy,— that 'tis the easiest thing in all the world for a man to drift away from God. Ay, or a woman either. You may do it, and never know that you have done it,—for a while, at least. David was two full years ere he found it out. Oh Dorothy, take warning! I was once as innocent as you are. I have drifted from God, oh my child, how far! The Lord keep you from a like fate.' I was fairly affrighted, for his face was terrible. An hour after, I saw him dealing the cards at ombre, with a look as bright and mirthful as though he knew not grief but by name."

Phoebe looked up with eyes full of meaning. "Did he never come back?"

"Dear child," said Mrs Dorothy, turning to her, "hast thou forgot that the Good Shepherd goeth after that which was lost, until He find it? He came back, my dear. But it was

Emily Sarah Holt

through the Great Plague and the Great Fire."

It was evident for a few minutes that Mrs Dorothy was wrestling with painful memories.

"Well, and what then?" said Rhoda, who wanted the story to go on, and was afraid of what she called preaching.

"Well!" resumed the old lady, more lightly, "then, for three days in the week I had a dancing-master come to teach me; and twice in the week a music-master; and all manner of new gowns, and my hair dressed in a multitude of curls; and my mother's maid to teach me French, and see that I carried myself well. And when this had gone on a while, my mother began to carry me a-visiting when she went to see her friends. For above a year she used a hackney coach; but then my father was made Doctor, and had a great church given him that was then all the mode; and my Lady Jennings came up to Town, and finding he had parts, she began to take note of him, and would carry him in her coach to the Court; and my mother would then set up her own coach, the which she did. And at length, the summer before I was one-and-twenty, my Lady Jennings, without the privity of my father, offered my mother to have me a maid to one of the Ladies in Waiting on the Queen. From this place, said she, if I played my cards well, and was liked of them above me, I might come in time to be a Maid of Honour."

"O rare!" exclaimed Rhoda. "And did you, Mrs Dolly?"

"Yes, child," slowly answered Mrs Dorothy. "I did so."

Rhoda's face was sparkling with interest and pleasure. Phoebe's was shadowed with forebodings, of a sad end to come.

"The night ere I left home for the Court," pursued the old lady, "my mother held long converse with me. 'Thou art mightily improved, Dolly,' saith she, 'since thy coming to London; but there is yet a stiff soberness about thee, that thou wilt do well to be rid of. Thou shouldst have more ease, child. Do but look at thy cousin Jenny, that is three years younger than thou, and yet how will she rattle to every man that hath a word of compliment to pay her!' But after she had made an end, my father called me into his closet. 'Poor Dorothy!' he said. 'The bloom is not all off the peach yet. But 'tis going, child—'tis fast going. I feared this. Poor Dorothy!'"

"Oh, dear!" said Rhoda. "You were not going to a funeral, Mrs Dolly!"

"Ah, child! maybe, if I had, it had been the better for me. The wise man saith, 'It is better to go to the house of mourning than to the house of feasting.'"

"But pray, what harm came to you, Mrs Dorothy?"

"No outward bodily harm at all, my dear. Yet even that was no thanks to me. It was 'of the Lord's compassion,' seeing He had a purpose of mercy toward me. But, ah me! what inward and spiritual harm! Mrs Rhoda, my dear, I saw sights and heard sayings those two years I dwelt in the Court which I would give the world, so to speak, only to forget them now."

"What were they, Mrs Dorothy?" asked Rhoda, eagerly sitting up.

"Think you I am likely to tell you, child? No, indeed!"

"But what sort of harm did they to you, Mrs Dolly?"

"Child, I learned to think lightly of sin. People did not talk of sin there at all; the words they used were crime and vice. Every wrong doing was looked on as it affected other men: if it touched your neighbour's purse or person, it was ill; if it only grieved his heart, then 'twas a little matter. But how it touched God was never so much as thought on. There might have been no God in Heaven, so little account was taken of Him there."

"Now do tell us. Mrs Dolly, what the Queen was like, and the King," said Rhoda, yawning. "And how many Maids of Honour were there? Just tell us all about it."

"There were six," replied the old lady, taking up her knitting, which she had dropped in her earnestness a minute before. "And Mrs Sanderson was their mother. I reckon you will scarce know that always a married gentlewoman goeth about with these young damsels, called the Mother of the Maids, whose work it is to see after them."

"And keep them from everything jolly!" exclaimed Rhoda. "Now, that's a shame! Wouldn't it be fun to bamboozle that creature? I protest I should enjoy it!"

"O Mrs Rhoda! Mrs Rhoda!"

"I should, of all things, Mrs Dolly! But now, what were the King and Queen like? Was she very beautiful?"

[Note: Charles the Second and Catherine of Braganza.]

"No," said Mrs Dorothy, "she was not. She had pretty feet, fine eyes, and very lovely hair. 'Twas rich brown on the top of her head, and descending downward it grew into jet black. For the rest, she was but tolerable. In truth, her teeth wronged her by sticking too far out of her mouth; but for that she would have been lovelier by much."

"Horrid!" said Rhoda. "I forget where she came from, Mrs Dolly?"

"She came from Portingale, my dear, being daughter to the King of that country, and her name was Catherine."

"And what was the King like?"

"When he was little, my dear, his mother, Queen Mary, used to say he was so ugly a baby that she was quite ashamed of him. He was better-favoured when he grew a man; he had good eyes, but a large Mouth."

[Note: Queen Mary was Henrietta Maria, always termed Queen Mary during her own reign.]

"He was a black man, was he not?"

By which term Rhoda meant what we now call a dark man.

"Yes, very black and swarthy."

"Where did he commonly live?"

"Mostly at Whitehall or Saint James's. At times he went to Hampton Court, and often, for a change of sir, to Newmarket; now and then to Tunbridge Wells. He was but little at Windsor."

"Did you like him, Mrs Dorothy?"

Phoebe looked up, when no answer came. The expression of Mrs Dorothy's face was a curious mixture of fear, repulsion, and yet amusement.

Emily Sarah Holt

"No!" she said at length.

"Why not?" demanded Rhoda.

"Well, there were some that did," was the reply, in a rather constrained tone; "and the one that he behaved the worst to loved him the best of all."

"How droll!" said Rhoda. "And who were your friends, then, Mrs Dorothy?"

"That depends, my dear, on what you mean by friends. If you mean them that flattered me, and joked with me, and the like,—why, I had very many; or if you mean them that would take some trouble to push me in the world,—well, there were several of those; but if you mean such as are only true friends, that would have cast one thought to my real welfare, whether I should go to Heaven or Hell,—I had but one of that sort."

"And who was your one friend, Mrs Dolly?" asked Rhoda, pursing up her lips a little.

"The King's Scots cook, my dear," quietly replied Mrs Dorothy.

"The *what*?" shrieked Rhoda, going into convulsions of laughter.

"Ah, you may laugh, Mrs Rhoda. You know there's an old saying, 'Let them laugh that win.' If ever an old sinner like me enters the gates of Heaven, so far as the human means are concerned, I shall owe it, first of all, to old David Armstrong."

"Will you please to tell us about him, Madam?" rather

timidly asked Phoebe.

"With all my heart, my dear. Dear old Davie! Methinks I see him now. Picture to yourselves, my dears, a short man, something stooping in the shoulders, with sharp features and iron-grey hair; always dressed in his white cooking garb, and a white cap over his frizzled locks. But before I tell you what I knew of old Davie, methinks I had better tell you a tale of him that will give you some diversion, without I mistake."

"Oh do, Mrs Dolly?" cried Rhoda, who feared nothing so much as too great seriousness in her friend's stones.

"Well," said Mrs Dorothy, "then you must know, my dears, that once upon a time the King and Queen were at dinner, and with them, amongst others, my Lord Rochester, who was at that time a very wild gallant. He died, indeed, very penitent, and, I trust, a saved man; but let that be. They were sat after dinner, and my Lord Rochester passes the bottle about to his next neighbour. 'Come, man!' saith the King, in his rollicksome way, 'take a glass of that which cheereth God and man, as Scripture saith.' My Lord Rochester at once bets the King forty pound that there was no such saying in Scripture. The King referreth all to the Queen's chaplain, that happened to be the only parson then present; but saith again, that though he could not name the place, yet he was as certain to have read it in Scripture as that his name was Charles, 'What thinks your Majesty?' quoth my Lord Rochester, turning to the Queen. She, very modestly—"

"But, Mrs Dolly, was not the Queen a Papist? What would she know about the Bible?"

"So she was, my dear. But they have a Bible of their own, that they allow the reading of to certain persons. And I dare say she was one. However, my Lord Rochester asked her, for

I heard him; and she said, very womanly, that she was unfit to decide such matters, but she could not think there to be any such passage in the Bible."

"Why, there isn't!" rashly interpolated Rhoda.

Mrs Dorothy smiled, but did not contradict her.

"Then up spoke the Queen's chaplain, and gave his voice like his mistress, that there was no such passage; and several others of them at the table said they thought the like. So the King, swearing his wonted oath, cried out for some to bring a Bible, that he might search and see."

"O Mrs Dolly! what was his favourite oath?"

"I do not see, my dear, that it would do you any good to know it. Well, the Bible, as matters went, was not to be had. King, Queen, chaplain, and courtiers, there was not a man nor woman at the table that owned to possessing a Bible."

"How shocking!" said Phoebe, under her breath.

"Very shocking, my dear," assented Mrs Dorothy. "But all at once my Lord Rochester cries out, 'Please your Majesty, I'll lay you forty shillings there's one man in this palace that has a Bible! He cut me short for swearing in the yard a month since. That's old David, your Majesty's Scots cook. If you'll send for him—' 'Done!' says the King. 'Killigrew, root out old Davie, and tell him to come here, and bring his Bible with him.' So away went Mr Killigrew, the King's favourite page; and ere long back he comes, and old Davie with him, and under Davie's arm a great brown book. 'Here he is, Sire, Bible and all!' says Mr Killigrew. 'Come forward, Davie, and be hanged!' says the King. 'I'll come forward, Sire, at your Majesty's bidding,' says Davie, 'and gin ye order it, and I ha'e deservit it, I can be hangit,' saith he, mighty dry; 'but under your Majesty's pleasure I'll just tak' the liberty to ask, Sire, what are ye wantin' wi' the Buik?"

"Oh, how queer you talk, Mrs Dolly!"

"As David talked, my dear. He was a Scot, you know. Well, the King gave a hearty laugh; and says he, 'Oh, come forward, Davie, and fear nothing. We'll not hang you, and we want no hurt to your darling book.' 'Atweel, Sire,' says Davie, 'and I'd ha'e been gey sorry gin ye had meant to hurt my buik, seein' it was my mither's, and I set store by it for her sake; but trust me, Sire, I'd ha'e been a hantle sorrier gin ye had meant onie disrespect to the Lord's Buik. I'll no stand by, wi' a' honour to your Majesty, an' see I lichtlied.'"

"What does that mean, Mrs Dolly?"

"Set light by, my dear. Well, the King laughed again, but I think Davie's words a little sobered him, for he spoke kindly enough, that no harm should be done, nor was any disrespect intended; 'but,' saith he, 'my Lord Rochester and I fell a-disputing if certain words were in the Bible or no; and as you are the only man here like to have one, I sent for you.' Davie looks, quiet enough, round all the table; and he says, under his breath, 'The only man here like to have a Bible! Ay, your Majesty, I ken weel eneuch that I ha'e my habitation among the tents o' Kedar. Atweel, Sire, an' I'll be pleasit to answer onie sic question, gin ye please to tell me the words.' My Lord Rochester saith, '"Wine, which cheereth God and man." Are such words as those in the Bible, David?' Neither yea nor nay said old Davie: but he turned over the leaves of his Bible for a moment, and then, clearing his voice, and first doffing his cook's cap (which he had but lifted a minute for the King), he read from the Book of Judges, Jotham's parable of the trees. 'Twas a little while ere any spoke: then said the

Queen's chaplain, swearing a great oath, that he could not but be infinitely surprised to find there to be such words in the Bible."

"O Mrs Dolly! a parson to swear!"

"There are different sorts of parsons, my dear. But old David thought it shocking, for he turns round to the chaplain, and saith he, 'Your pardon, Mr Howard, but gin ye'd give me leave, I'd be pleasit to swear the neist oath for ye. It would sound rather better, ye ken, for a cook than a chaplain.' 'Hurrah!' says the King, swearing himself, 'the sprightliest humour I heard of a long time! Pray you, silence, and hear old Davie swear!' 'I see nothing to swear anent the now, an' it please your Majesty,' says Davie, mighty dry again: 'when I do, your Majesty'll be sure to hear it.' The King laughed heartily, for he took Davie right enough, though I saw some look puzzled. Of course he never would see reason to do a sinful thing. But a new thought had come into the King's head, and he turns quick to Mr Howard, and desires that he would give exposition of the words that Davie had read. 'You ought to know what they mean, if we don't, poor sinners,' saith the King. 'I protest, Sire,' saith the chaplain, 'that I cannot so much as guess what they mean.' 'Now then, David the divine,' cries my Lord Rochester, 'your exposition, if you please.' And some of the courtiers, that by this time were not too sober, drummed on the table with glasses, and shouted for David's sermon."

"I think, Mrs Dolly, that was scarce proper, in the King's and Queen's presence."

"So I think, my dear. But King Charles's Court was Liberty Hall, and every man did that which was right in his own eyes. But Davie stood very quiet, with the Bible yet open in his hands. He waited his master's bidding, if they did not. 'Oh ay, go on, Davie,' saith the King, leaning back in his chair and laughing. 'Silence for Mr David Armstrong's sermon!' cries my Lord Rochester, in a voice of a master of ceremonies. But Davie took no note of any voice but the King's, though 'twas to my Lord Rochester he addressed him when he spoke. 'That wine cheereth man, your Lordship very well knows,' quoth Davie, in his dry way: and seeing his Lordship had drank a bottle and a half since he sat down, I should think he did, my dears. 'But this, that wine cheereth God, is referable to the drink-offering commanded by God of the Jews, wherein the wine doth seem to typify the precious blood of Christ, and the thankfulness of him that hath his iniquity thereby purged away. For in the fifteenth chapter of the Book of Numbers you shall find this drink-offering termed "a sweet savour unto the Lord." And since nothing but Christ is a sweet savour unto God, therefore we judge that the wine of the drink-offering, like to that of the Sacrament, did denote the blood of Christ whereby we are redeemed; the one prefiguring that whereto it looked forward, as the other doth likewise figure that whereunto it looketh back. This, therefore, that wine cheereth God, is to be understood by an emblem, of the blood of Christ, our Mediator; for through this means God is well pleased in the way of salvation that He hath appointed, whereby His justice is satisfied. His law fulfilled, His mercy reigneth, His grace doth triumph, all His perfections do agree together, the sinner is saved, and God in Christ glorified. Now, Sire, I have done your bidding, and I humbly ask your Majesty's leave to withdraw.' The King said naught, but cast him a nod of consent. My dears, you never saw such a change as had come over that table. Every man seemed sobered and awed. The Queen was weeping, the King silent and thoughtful. My Lord Rochester, whom at that time nothing could sober long, was the only one to speak, and rising with make-believe gravity, as though in his place in the House of Lords, he offered a motion that the King should please to send Mr

Howard into the kitchen to make kail, and raise the Reverend Mr David Armstrong to the place of chaplain."

"What is kail, Mrs Dolly?" asked Rhoda, laughing.

"'Tis Scots broth, my dear, whereof King Charles was very fond, and old David had been fetched from Scotland on purpose to make it for him."

"What a droll old man!" exclaimed Rhoda.

"Ah, he was one of the best men ever I knew," said Mrs Dorothy. "But, my dear, look at the clock!"

"I declare!" cried Rhoda. "Phoebe, we have but just time to run home ere supper, if so much as that. Good evening, Mrs Dolly, and thank you. What will Madam say?"

* * * * *

Note: David Armstrong is a historical person, and this anecdote is true. The surname given to him only is fictitious, as history does not record any name but "David."

CHAPTER FOUR

THROUGH THORNY PATHS

"I do repent me now too late of each impatient thought,
That would not let me tarry out God's leisure as I ought."

Caroline Bowles.

"Is it long since Madam woke, Baxter?" cried Rhoda in a breathless whisper, as she came in at the side door.

"But this minute, Mrs Rhoda," answered he.

"That's good!" said Rhoda aside to Phoebe, and slipping off her shoes, she ran lightly and silently upstairs, beckoning her cousin to follow.

Phoebe, having no idea of the course of Rhoda's thoughts, obeyed, and followed her example in doffing her hood and smoothing her hair.

"Be quick!" said Rhoda, her own rapid movements over, and putting on her shoes again.

They found Madam looking barely awake, and staring hard at her book, as if wishful to persuade herself that she had

Emily Sarah Holt

been reading.

"I hope, child, you were not out all this time," said she to Rhoda.

"Oh no, Madam!" glibly answered that trustworthy young lady. "We only had a dish of tea with Mrs Dolly, and I made my compliments to the other gentlewomen."

"And where were you since, child?"

"We have been upstairs, Madam," said Rhoda, unblushingly.

"Not diverting yourselves, I hope?" was Madam's next question.

"Oh no, not at all, Madam. We were not doing anything particular."

"Talking, I suppose, as maids will," responded Madam. "Phoebe, to-morrow after breakfast bring all your clothes to my chamber. I must have you new apparelled."

"Oh, Madam, give me leave to come also!" exclaimed Rhoda, with as much eagerness as she ever dared to show in her grandmother's presence. "I would so dearly like to hear what Phoebe is to have! Only, please, not a musk-coloured damask—you promised me that."

"My dear," answered Madam, "you forget yourself. I cannot talk of such things to-day. You may come if you like."

Supper was finished in silence. After supper, a pale-faced, tired-looking young man, who had been previously invisible, came into the parlour, and made a low reverence to Madam, which she returned with a queenly bend of her head. His black cassock and scarf showed him to be in holy orders. Madam rang the hand-bell, the servants filed in, and evening prayers were read by the young chaplain, in a thin, monotonous voice, with a manner which indicated that he was not interested himself, and did not expect interest in any one else. Then the servants filed out again; the chaplain kissed Madam's hand, and wished her good-night, bowed distantly to Rhoda, half bowed to Phoebe, instantly drew himself up as if he thought he was making a mistake, and finally disappeared.

"'Tis time you were abed, maids," said Madam.

Rhoda somewhat slowly rose, knelt before her grandmother, and kissed her hand.

"Good-night, my dear. God bless thee, and make thee a good maid!" was Madam's response.

Phoebe had risen, and stood, rather hesitatingly, behind her cousin. She was doubtful whether Madam would be pleased or displeased if she followed Rhoda's example. In her new life it seemed probable that she would not be short of opportunities for the exercise of meekness, forbearance, and humility. Madam's quick eyes detected Phoebe's difficulty in an instant.

"Good-night, Phoebe," she said, rising.

"Good-night, Madam," replied Phoebe in a low voice, as she followed Rhoda. It was evident that no relationship was to be recognised.

"Here, you carry the candle," said Rhoda, nodding towards the hall table on which the candlesticks stood. "That's what you are here for, I suppose,—to save me trouble. Dear, I forgot my cloak,—see where it is! Bring it with you, Phoebe."

Demurely enough Rhoda preceded Phoebe upstairs. But no sooner was the bedroom door closed behind them, than Rhoda threw herself into the large invalid chair, and laughed with hearty amusement.

"Oh, didn't I take her in? Wasn't it neatly done, now? Didn't you admire me, Phoebe?"

"You told her a lie!" retorted Phoebe, indignantly.

"'Sh!—that's not a pretty word," said Rhoda, pursing her lips. "Say a fib, next time.—Nonsense! Not a bit of it, Phoebe. We had been upstairs since we came in."

"Only a minute," answered Phoebe. "You made her think what was not true. Father called that a lie,—I don't know what you call it."

"Now, Phoebe," said Rhoda severely, "don't you be a little Puritan. If you set up for a saint at White-Ladies, I can just tell you, you'll pull your own nest about your ears. You are mightily mistaken if you think Madam has any turn for saints. She reckons them designing persons—every soul of 'em. You'll just get into a scrape if you don't have a care."

Phoebe made no reply. She was standing by the window, looking up into the darkened sky. There were no blinds at White-Ladies.

It was well for Rhoda—or was it well?—that she could not just then see into Phoebe's heart. The cry that "shivered to the tingling stars" was unheard by her. "O Father, Father," said the cry. "Why did you die and leave your poor little

Phoebe, whom nobody loves, whose love nobody wants, with whom nobody here has one feeling in common?" And then all at once came as it were a vision before her eyes, of a scene whereof she had heard very frequently from her father,—a midnight meeting of the Desert Church, in a hollow of the Cevennes mountains, guarded by sentinels posted on the summit,—a meeting which to attend was to brave the gallows or the galleys,—and Phoebe fancied she could hear the words of the opening hymn, as the familiar tune floated past her:—

"Mon sort n'est pas a plaindre, Il est a desirer; Je n'ai plus rien a craindre, Car Dieu est mon Berger."

It was a quiet, peaceful face which was turned back to Rhoda.

"Did you hear?" rather sharply demanded that young lady.

"Yes, I heard what you said," calmly replied Phoebe. "But I have been a good way since."

"A good way!—where?" rejoined her cousin.

"To France and back," said Phoebe, with a smile.

"What are you talking about?" stared Rhoda. "I said nothing about France; I was telling you not to be a prig and a saint, and make Madam angry."

"I won't vex her if I can help it," answered Phoebe.

"Well, but you will, if you set up to be better than your neighbours,—that's pos.! Take the pins out of my commode."

Emily Sarah Holt

"Why should not I be better than my neighbours?" asked Phoebe, as she pulled out the pins.

"Because they'll all hate you—that's why. I must have clean ruffles—they are in that top drawer."

"Aren't you better than your neighbours?" innocently suggested Phoebe, coming back with the clean ruffles.

Rhoda paused to consider how she should deal with the subject. The question was not an easy one to answer. She believed herself very much better, in every respect: to say No, therefore, would belie her wishes and convictions; yet to say Yes, would spoil the effect of her lecture. There was moreover, a dim impression on her mind that Phoebe was incapable of perceiving the delicate distinction between them, which made it inevitable that Rhoda should be better than Phoebe, and highly indecorous that Phoebe should attempt to be better than Rhoda. On the whole, it seemed desirable to turn the conversation.

"Oh, not these ruffles, Phoebe! These are some of my best. Bring a pair of common ones—those with the box plaits.— What were you thinking about France?"

"Oh, nothing particular. I was only—"

"Never mind, if you don't want to tell," said Rhoda, graciously, now that her object was attained. "I wonder what new clothes Madam will give you. A camlet for best, I dare say, and duffel for every day. Don't you want to know?"

"No, not very much."

"I should, if I were you. I like to go fine. Not that she'll give *you* fine things, you know—not likely. There! put my shoes out to clean, and tuck me up nicely, and then if you like you can go to bed. I shan't want anything more."

Phoebe did as she was requested, and then knelt down.

"I vow!" exclaimed her cousin, when she rose. "Do you say your prayers on Sunday nights? I never do. Why, we've only just been at it downstairs. And what a time you are! I'm never more than five minutes with mine!"

"I couldn't say all I want in five minutes," replied Phoebe.

"Want! why, what do you want?" said Rhoda. "I want nothing. I've got to do it—that's all."

"Well, I dare say five minutes is enough for that," was the quiet reply from Phoebe. "But when people get into trouble, then they do want things."

"Trouble! Oh, you don't know!" said Rhoda, loftily. "I've had heaps of trouble."

"Have you?" innocently demanded Phoebe, in an interested tone.

"Well, I should think so! More than ever you had."

"What were they?" said Phoebe, in the same manner.

"Why, first, my mother died when I was only a week old," explained Rhoda. "I suppose, you call that a trouble?"

"Not when you were a week old," said Phoebe; "it would be afterwards—with some people. But I should not think it was, much, with you. You have had Madam."

"Well, then my father went off to London, and spent all his estate, that I should have had, and there was nothing left for me. That was a trouble, I suppose?"

"If you had plenty beside, I should not think it was."

"'Plenty beside!' Phoebe, you are the silliest creature! Why, don't you see that I should have been a great fortune, if I had had Peveril as well as White-Ladies? I should have set my cap at a lord, I can tell you. Only think, Phoebe, I should have had sixty thousand pounds. What do you say to that? Sixty thousand pounds!"

"I should think it is more than you could ever spend."

"Oh, I don't know about that," said Rhoda. "When White-Ladies is mine, I shall have a riding-horse and a glass coach; and I will have a splendid set of diamonds, and pearls too. They cost something, I can tell you. Oh, 'tis easy spending money. You'll see, when it comes to me."

"Are you sure it will come to you?"

"Why, of course it will!" exclaimed Rhoda, sitting up, and leaning on her elbow. "To whom else would Madam leave it, I should like to know! Why, you never expect her to give it to *you*, poor little white-faced thing? I vow, but that is a good jest!"

Rhoda's laugh had more bitterness than mirth in it. Phoebe's smile was one of more unmixed amusement.

"Pray make yourself easy," said Phoebe. "I never expect anything, and then I am not disappointed."

"Well, I'll just tell you what!" rejoined her cousin. "If I catch you making up to Madam, trying to please all her whims, and chime in with her vapours, and that—fancying she'll leave you White-Ladies—I tell you, Phoebe Latrobe, I'll never forgive you as long as I live! There!"

Rhoda was very nearly, if not quite, in a passion. Phoebe turned and looked at her.

"Cousin," she said, gently, "you will see me try to please Madam, since 'tis my duty: but if you suppose 'tis with any further object, such as what she might give me, you very ill know Phoebe Latrobe."

"Well, mind your business!" said Rhoda, rather fiercely.

A few minutes later she was asleep. But sleep did not visit Phoebe's eyes that night.

When the morning came, Rhoda seemed quite to have forgotten her vexation. She chattered away while she was dressing, on various topics, but chiefly respecting the new clothes which Madam had promised to Phoebe. If words might be considered a criterion, Rhoda appeared to take far more interest in these than Phoebe herself.

Breakfast was a solemn and silent ceremony. When it was over, Madam desired Phoebe to attend her in her own chamber, and to bring her wardrobe with her. Rhoda followed, unasked, and sat down on the form at the foot of the bed to await her cousin. Phoebe came in with her arms full of dresses and cloaks. She was haunted by a secret apprehension which she would not on any account have put into words—that she might no longer be allowed to wear mourning for her dead father. But Phoebe's fears were super-fluous. Madam thought far too much of the proprieties of life to commit such an indecorum. However little she had liked

Emily Sarah Holt

or respected the Rev. Charles Latrobe, she would never have thought of requiring his child to lay aside her mourning until the conventional two years had elapsed from the period of his decease.

Phoebe's common attire was very quickly discarded, as past further wear; and she was desired to wear her best clothes every day, until new ones were ready for her. This decided, Rhoda was ordered to ring for Betty, Madam's own maid, and Betty was in her turn required to fetch those stuffs which she had been bidden to lay aside till needed. Betty accordingly brought a piece of black camlet, another of black bombazine, and a third of black satin, with various trimmings. The two girls alike watched in silence, while Betty measured lengths and cut off pieces of camlet and bombazine, from which it appeared that Phoebe was to have two new dresses, and a mantua and hood of the camlet: but when Rhoda heard Betty desired to cut off satin for another mantua, her hitherto concealed chagrin broke forth.

"Why, Madam!—she'll be as fine as me!"

"My dear, she will be as I choose," answered Madam, in a tone which would have silenced any one but Rhoda. "And now, satin for a hood, Betty—"

"'Tis a shame!" said Rhoda, under her breath, which was as much as she dared venture; but Madam took no notice.

"You will line the hoods and mantuas warm, Betty," pursued Madam, in her most amiable tone. "Guard the satin with fur, and the camlet with that strong gimp. And a muff she must have, Betty."

"A muff!" came in a vexed whisper from Rhoda.

"And when the time comes, one of the broidered India scarves that were had of Staveley, for summer wear; but that anon. Then—"

"But, Madam!" put in Rhoda, in a troubled voice, "you have never given me one of those scarves yet! I asked you for one a year ago." To judge from her tone, Rhoda was very near tears.

"My dear!" replied Madam, "'tis becoming in maids to wait till they are spoken to. Had you listened with proper respect, you would have heard me bid Betty lay out one also for you. You cannot use them at this season."

Rhoda subsided, somewhat discontentedly.

"Two pairs of black Spanish gloves, Betty; and a black fan, and black velvet stays. (When the year is out she must have a silver lace.) And bid Dobbins send up shoes to fit on, with black buckles—two pairs; and lay out black stockings—two pairs of silk, and two of worsted; and plain cambric aprons— they may be laced when the year is out. I think that is all. Oh!—a fur tippet, Betty."

And with this last order Madam marched away.

"Oh, shocking!" cried Rhoda, the instant she thought her grandmother out of hearing. "I vow, but she's going to have you as fine as me. Every bit of it. Betty, isn't it a shame?"

"Well, no, Mrs Rhoda, I don't see as how 'tis," returned Betty, bluntly. "Mrs Phoebe, she's just the same to Madam as you are."

"But she isn't!" exclaimed Rhoda, blazing up. "I'm her eldest daughter's child, and she's only the youngest. And she hasn't

Emily Sarah Holt

done it before, neither. Last night she didn't let her kiss her hand. I say, Betty, 'tis a crying shame!"

"Maybe Madam thought better of it this morning," suggested Betty, speaking with a pin in her mouth.

"Well, 'tis a burning shame!" growled Rhoda.

"Perhaps, Mrs Betty," said Phoebe's low voice, "you could leave the satin things for a little while?"

"Mrs Phoebe, I durstn't, my dear!" rejoined Betty; "nay, not if 'twas ever so! Madam, she's used to have folk do as she bids 'em; and she'll make 'em, too! Never you lay Mrs Rhoda's black looks to heart, my dear, she'll have forgot all about it by this time to-morrow."

Rhoda had walked away.

"But I shall not!" answered Phoebe, softly.

"Deary me, child!" said Betty, turning to look at her, "don't you go for to fret over that. Why, if a bit of a thing like that'll trouble you, you'll have plenty to fret about at White-Ladies. Mrs Rhoda, she's on and off with you twenty times a day; and you'd best take no notice. She don't mean anything ill, my dear; 'tis only her phantasies."

"Oh, Mrs Betty! I wish—"

"Phoebe!" came up from below. "Fetch my cloak and hood, and bring your own—quick, now! We are about to drive out with Madam."

"Come, dry your eyes, child, and I'll fetch the things," said Betty, soothingly. "You'll be the better of a drive."

Rhoda's annoyance seemed to have vanished from her mind as well as from her countenance; and Madam took no notice of Phoebe's disturbed looks. The Maidens' Lodge, was first visited, and a messenger sent in to ask Lady Betty if she were inclined to take the air. Lady Betty accepted the offer, and was so considerate as not to keep Madam wailing more than ten minutes. No further invitation was offered, and the coach rumbled away in the direction of Gloucester.

For a time Phoebe heard little of the conversation between the elder ladies, and Rhoda, as usual in her grandmother's presence, was almost silent. At length she woke up to a remark made by Lady Betty.

"Then you think, Madam, to send for Gatty and Molly?"

"That is my design, my Lady Betty. 'Twill be a diversion for Rhoda; and Sir Richard was so good as to say they should come if I would."

"Indeed, I think he would be easy to have them from home, Madam, till they may see if Betty's disorder be the small-pox or no."

"When did Betty return home, my Lady?"

"But last Tuesday. 'Tis not possible that her sisters have taken aught of her, for she had been ailing some days ere she set forth, and they have bidden at home all the time. You will be quite safe, Madam."

"So I think, my Lady Betty," replied Madam. "Rhoda, have you been listening?"

"No, Madam," answered Rhoda, demurely.

Emily Sarah Holt

"Then 'tis time you should, my dear," said Madam, graciously. "I will acquaint you of the affair. I think to write to Lady Delawarr, and ask the favour of Mrs Gatty and Mrs Molly to visit me. Their sister Mrs Betty, as I hear, is come home from the Bath, extreme distempered; and 'tis therefore wise to send away Mrs Gatty and little Mrs Molly until Mrs Betty be recovered of her disorder. I would have you be very nice toward them, that they shall find their visit agreeable."

"How long will they stay, Madam?" inquired Rhoda.

"Why, child, that must hang somewhat on Mrs Betty's recovering. I take it, it shall be about a month; but should her distemper be tardy of disappearing, it shall then be something longer."

"Jolly!" was the sound which seemed to Phoebe to issue in an undertone from the lips of Rhoda. But the answer which reached her grandmother's ears was merely a sedate "Yes, Madam."

"I take it, my Lady Betty," observed Madam, turning to her companion, "that the sooner the young gentlewomen are away, the better shall it be."

"Oh, surely, Madam!" answered Lady Betty. "'Tis truly very good of you to ask it; but you are always a general undertaker for your friends."

"We were sent into this world to do good, my Lady Betty," returned Madam, sententiously.

Unless Phoebe's ears were deceived, a whisper very like "Fudge!" came from Rhoda.

The somewhat solemn drive was finished at last; Lady Betty

was set down at the Maidens' Lodge; inquiries were made as to the health of Mrs Marcella, who returned a reply intimating that she was a suffering martyr; and Rhoda and Phoebe at last found themselves free from superveillance, and safe in their bedroom.

"Now that's just jolly!" was Rhoda's first remark, with nothing in particular to precede it. "Molly Delawarr's a darling! I don't much care for Gatty, and Betty I just hate. She's a prig and a fid-fad both. But Molly—oh, Phoebe, she's as smart as can be. Such parts she has! You know, she's really—not quite you understand—but really she's almost as clever as I am!"

Phoebe did not seem overwhelmed by this information; she only said, "Is she?"

"Well, nearly," said Rhoda. "She knows fourteen Latin words, Molly does; and she always brings them in."

"Into what?" asked Phoebe, with the little amused laugh which was very rare with her.

"Into her discourse, to be sure, child!" said Rhoda, loftily, "You don't know fourteen Latin words; how should you?"

"How should I, indeed," rejoined Phoebe, meekly, "if father had not taught me?"

"Taught you—taught you Latin?" gasped Rhoda.

"Just a little Latin and Greek; there wasn't time for much," humbly responded Phoebe.

"Greek!" shrieked Rhoda.

"Very little, please," deprecated Phoebe.

"Phoebe, you dear sweet darling love of a Phoebe!" cried Rhoda, kissing her cousin, to the intense astonishment of the latter; "now won't you, like a dear as you are, just tell me one or two Greek words? I would give anything to outshine Molly and make her look foolish, I would! She doesn't know one word of Greek—only Latin. Do, for pity's sake, tell me, if 'tis only one Greek word! and I won't say another syllable, not if Madam gives you a diamond necklace!"

Phoebe was laughing more than she had yet ever done at White-Ladies. She was far too innocent and amiable to think of playing Rhoda the trick of which Melanie's father was guilty, in *Contes a ma Fille*, when, under the impression that she was saying in Latin, "Knowledge gives the right to laugh at everything," he cruelly caused her to remark in public, "I am a very ridiculous donkey." Phoebe bore no malice. She only said, still smiling, "I don't know what words to tell you."

"Oh, any!" answered Rhoda, accommodatingly. "What's the Greek for ugly?"

"I don't know," said Phoebe, dubiously. "Kakos means *bad*."

"And what is *good* and *pretty*?"

"Agathos is *good*," replied Phoebe, laughing; "and *beautiful* is kallios."

"That'll do!" said Rhoda, triumphantly. "'Tis plenty,—I couldn't remember more. Let me see,—kaks, and agathos, and kallius—is that right?"

Phoebe laughingly offered the necessary corrections. "All

right!" said Rhoda. "I've no more to wish for. I'll take the shine out of Molly!"

At supper that evening, Madam announced that she had sent her note to Lady Delawarr by a mounted messenger, and had received an answer, according to which Gatty and Molly might be expected to arrive at White-Ladies on Wednesday evening. Madam appeared to be in one of her most gracious moods, for she even condescended to inform Phoebe that Mrs Gatty was two months older than Rhoda, and Mrs Molly four years her junior,—"two years younger than you, my dear," said Madam, very affably.

"Now, Phoebe, I'll tell you what we'll do," asserted Rhoda, as she sat down before the glass that night to have her hair undressed by her cousin. "I'm not going to have Molly teasing about the old gentlewomen down yonder. I'll soon shut her mouth if she begins; and if Gatty wants to go down there, well, she can go by herself. So I'll tell you what: you and I will drink a dish of tea with Mrs Dolly to-morrow, and we'll make her finish her story. I only do wish the dear old tiresome thing wouldn't preach! Then I'll take you in to see Mrs Marcella, and we'll get that done. Then in the morning, you must just set out all my gowns on the bed, and I'll have both you and Betty to sew awhile I must have some lace on that blue. I'll make Madam give me a pair of new silver buckles, too. I can't do unless I cut out those creatures somehow. And the only way to cut out Gatty is by dress, because she hasn't anything in her,—'tis all on her. I cut out Molly in brains. But my Lady Delawarr likes to dress Gatty up, because she fancies the awkward thing's pretty. She isn't, you know,—not a speck; but *she* thinks so."

Whether the last pronoun referred to Lady Delawarr or to Gatty, Rhoda was not sufficiently perspicuous to indicate. Phoebe went on disentangling her hair in silence, and Rhoda likewise fell into a brown study.

Of the nature of her thoughts that young lady gave but two intimations: the first, as she tied up her hair in the loose bag which then served for a night-cap,—

"I cannot abide that Betty!"

The second came a long while afterwards, just as Phoebe was dropping to sleep.

"I say, Phoebe!"

"Yes?"

"Did you say 'kakios?'"

Phoebe had to collect her thoughts. "Kakos," she said.

"Oh, all right; *they* won't know. But won't I take the shine out of that Molly!"

Phoebe's arrested sleep came back to her as she was reflecting on the curious idea which her cousin seemed to have of friendship.

"Come along, Phoebe! This is the shortest way."

"Oh, couldn't we go by the road?" asked Phoebe, drawing back apprehensively, as Rhoda sprang lightly from the top of the stile which led into the meadow.

"Of course we could, but 'tis ever so much further round, and not half so pleasant. Why?"

"There are—cows!" said Phoebe, under her breath.

Rhoda laughed more decidedly than civilly.

"Cows! Did you never see cows before? I say, Phoebe, come along! Don't be so silly!"

Phoebe obeyed, but in evident trepidation, and casting many nervous glances at the dreaded cows, until the girls had passed the next stile.

"Cows don't bite, silly Phoebe!" said Rhoda, rather patronisingly, from the height of her two years' superiority in age.

"But they toss sometimes, don't they?" tremblingly demanded Phoebe.

"What nonsense!" said Rhoda, as they rounded the Maidens' Lodge.

Little Mrs Dorothy sat sewing at her window, and she nodded cheerily to her young guests as they came in.

"What do you think, Mrs Dolly?—good evening!" said Rhoda, parenthetically. "If this foolish Phoebe isn't frighted of a cow!"

"Sure, my dear, that is no wonder, for one bred in in the town," gently deprecated Mrs Dorothy.

"So stupid and nonsensical!" said Rhoda. "I say, Mrs Dolly, are you afraid of anything?"

"Yes, my dear," was the quiet answer.

"Oh!" said Rhoda. "Cows?"

"No, not cows," returned Mrs Dorothy, smiling.

"Frogs? Beetles?" suggested Rhoda.

"I do not think I am afraid of any animal, at least in this country, without it be vipers," said Mrs Dorothy. "But—well, I dare say I am but a foolish old woman in many regards. I oft fear things which I note others not to fear at all."

"But what sort of things, Mrs Dolly?" inquired Rhoda, who had made herself extremely comfortable with a large chair and sundry cushions.

"I will tell you of three things, my dear, of which I have always felt afraid, at the least since I came to years of discretion. And most folks are not afraid of any of them. I am afraid of getting rich. I am afraid of being married. And I am afraid of judging my neighbours."

"Oh!" cried Rhoda, in genuine amazement. "Why, Mrs Dolly, what *do* you mean? As to judging one's neighbours,— well, I suppose the Bible says something against that; but we all do it, you know."

"We do, my dear; more's the pity."

"But getting rich, and being married! Oh, Mrs Dolly! Every-body wants those."

"No, my dear, asking your pardon," replied the old lady, in a tone of decision unusual with her. "I trust every Christian does not want to be rich, when the Lord hath given him so many warnings against it. And every man does not want to marry, nor every woman neither."

"Well, not every man, perhaps," admitted Rhoda; "but every woman does, Mrs Dolly."

"My dear, I am sorry to hear a woman say it," answered Mrs Dorothy, with as much warmth as was consonant with her nature. "I hoped that was a man's delusion."

"Why, Mrs Dolly! I do," said Rhoda, with great candour.

"Then I wish you more wisdom, child."

"Well, upon my word!" exclaimed Rhoda. "Didn't you, when you were young, Mrs Dolly?"

"No, I thank God, nor when I was old neither," replied Mrs Dorothy, in the same tone.

"But, Mrs Dolly! A maid has no station in society!" said Rhoda, using a phrase which she had picked up from one of her grandfather's books.

"My dear, your station is where God puts you. A maid has just as good a station as a wife; and a much pleasanter, to my thinking."

"Pleasanter!" exclaimed Rhoda. "Why, Mrs Dolly, nobody thinks anything of an old maid, except to pity her."

"They may keep their pity to themselves," said Mrs Dorothy, with a little laugh. "We old maids can pity them back again, and with more reason."

"Mrs Dolly, would you have all the world hermits?"

"No, my dear; nor do I at all see why people should always leap to the conclusion that an old maid must be an ill-tempered, lonely, disappointed creature. Sure, there are other relatives in this world beside husbands and children; and if she choose her own lot, what cause hath she for

Emily Sarah Holt

disappointment? 'Tis but a few day since Mr Leighton said, in my hearing, 'Of course we know, when a gentlewoman is unwed, 'tis her misfortune rather than her fault'—and I do believe the poor man thought he paid us women a compliment in so speaking. For me, I felt it an insult."

"Why so, Mrs Dolly?"

"Why, think what it meant, my dear. 'Of course, a woman cannot be so insensible to the virtues and attractions of men that she should wish to remain unwed; therefore, if this calamity overtake her, it shows that she hath no virtues nor attractions herself.'"

"You don't think Mr Leighton meant that, Mrs Dolly?" asked Rhoda, laughing.

"No, my dear; I think he did not see the meaning of his own words. But tell me, if it is not a piece of great vanity on the part of men, that while they never think to condole with a man who is unmarried, but take it undoubted that he prefers that life, they take it as equally undoubted that a woman doth not prefer it, and lament over her being left at ease and liberty as though she had suffered some great misfortune?"

"I never did see such queer notions as you have, Mrs Dolly! I can't think where you get them," said Rhoda. "However, you may say what you will; *I* mean to marry, and I am going to be rich too. And I expect I shall like both of them."

"My dear!" and Mrs Dorothy laid down her work, and looked earnestly at Rhoda. "How do you know you are going to be rich?"

"Why, I shall have White-Ladies," answered Rhoda. "And of course Aunt Harriet will leave me everything."

"Have Madam and Mrs Harriet told you so, my dear?"

"No," said Rhoda, rather impatiently. "But who else should they leave it to?"

Mrs Dorothy let that part of the matter drop quietly.

"'They that will be rich fall into temptation and a snare,'" she said, taking up her work again.

"What snare?" said Rhoda, bluntly.

"They get their hearts choked up," said the old lady.

"With what, Mrs Dolly?"

"'Cares, and riches, and pleasures of this life.' O my dear, may the Lord make your heart soft! Yet I am afraid—I am very sore afraid, that the only way of making some hearts soft is—to break them."

"Well, I don't want my heart breaking, thank you," laughed Rhoda; "and I don't think anything would break it, unless I lost all my money, and was left an old maid. O Mrs Dolly, I can't think how you bear it! To come down, now, and live in one of these little houses, and have people looking down on you, instead of looking up to you—if anything of the sort would kill me, I think that would."

"Well, it hasn't killed me, child," said Mrs Dorothy, calmly; "but then, you see, I chose it. That makes a difference."

"But you didn't choose to be poor, Mrs Dolly?"

"Well, yes, in one sense, I did," answered the old lady, a little tinge of colour rising in her pale cheek.

"How so?" demanded Rhoda, who was not deterred from gaining information by any delicacy in asking questions.

"There was a time once, my dear, that I might have married a gentleman of title, with a rent-roll of six thousand a year."

"Mrs Dolly! you don't mean that?" cried Rhoda. "And why on earth didn't you?"

"Well, my dear, I had two reasons," answered Mrs Dorothy. "One was"—with a little laugh—"that as you see, I preferred to be one of these same ill-conditioned, lonely, disappointed old maids. And the other was"—and Mrs Dorothy's voice sank to a softer and graver tone—"I could not have taken my Master with me into that house. I saw no track of His footsteps along that road. And His sheep follow Him."

"But God means us to be happy, Mrs Dolly?"

"Surely, my dear. But He knows better than we how empty and fleeting is all happiness other than is found in Him. 'Tis only because the Lord is our Shepherd that we shall not want."

"Mrs Dolly, that is what good people say; but it always sounds so gloomy and melancholy."

"What sounds melancholy, my dear?" inquired Mrs Dorothy, with slight surprise in her tone.

"Why, that one must find all one's happiness in reading sermons, and chanting Psalms, and thinking how soon one is going to die," said Rhoda, with an uncomfortable shrug.

"My dear!" exclaimed Mrs Dorothy, "when did you ever hear me say anything of the kind?"

"Why, that was what you meant, wasn't it," answered Rhoda, "when you talked about finding happiness in piety?"

"And when did I do that?"

"Just now, this minute back," said Rhoda in surprise.

"My dear child, you strangely misapprehend me. I never spoke a word of finding happiness in piety; I spoke of finding it in God. And God is not sermons, nor chanting, nor death. He is life, and light, and love. I never think how soon I shall die. I often think how soon the Lord may come; but there is a vast difference between looking for the coming of a thing that you dread, and looking for the coming of a person whom you long to see."

"But you will die, Mrs Dolly?"

"Perhaps, my dear. The Lord may come first; I hope so."

"Oh dear!" said Rhoda. "But that means the world may come to an end."

"Yes. The sooner the better," replied the old lady.

"But you don't *want* the world to end, Mrs Dolly?"

"I do, my clear. I want the new heavens and the new earth, wherein dwelleth righteousness."

"Oh dear!" cried Rhoda again. "Why, Mrs Dolly, I can't bear to think of it. It would be an end of everything I care about."

"My dear," said the old lady, gravely and yet tenderly, "if the Lord's coming will put an end to everything you care about, that must be because you don't care much for Him."

Emily Sarah Holt

"I don't know anything about Him, except what we hear in church," answered Rhoda uneasily.

"And don't care for that?" softly responded her old friend.

Rhoda fidgeted for a moment, and then let the truth out.

"Well, no, Mrs Dolly, I *don't*. I know it sounds very wicked and shocking; but how can I, when 'tis all so far off? It doesn't feel real, as you do, and Madam, and all the other people I know. I can't tell how you make it real."

"*He* makes it real, my child. 'Tis faith which sees God. How can you see Him without it? But I am not shocked, my dear. You have only told me what I knew before."

"I don't see how you knew," said Rhoda uncomfortably; "and I don't know how people get faith."

"By asking the Lord for it," said Mrs Dolly. "Phoebe, my child, is it a sorrowful thing to thee to think on Christ and His coming again?"

"Oh no!" was Phoebe's warm answer. "You see, Madam, I haven't anything else."

"Dear child, thank God for it!" replied Mrs Dorothy softly. "'Ton sort n'est pas a plaindre.'"

"I declare, if 'tis not four o'clock!" cried Rhoda, springing up, and perhaps not sorry for the diversion. "There, now! I meant you to finish your story, and we haven't time left. Come along, Phoebe! We are going to look in a minute on Mrs Marcella, and then we must hurry home."

CHAPTER FIVE

GATTY'S TROUBLES

"And I come down no more to chilling praise,
To sneers, to wearing out of empty days,
But rest, rejoicing in the power I've won,
To go on learning, though my crying's done."

Isabella Fyvie Mayo.

As the two girls turned into the little garden of Number Three, the latch of the door was lifted, and Mrs Jane came out.

"Good evening!" said she. "Come to see my sister, are you? I and my Deb are doing for her to-day, for her Nell has got a holiday—gone to see her mother—lazy slut!"

"Which is the lazy slut, Mrs Jane?" asked Rhoda, laughing.

"Heyday! they're all a parcel together," answered Mrs Jane. "Nell and her mother, and her grandmother before them. And Marcella, too, she's no better. Go in, if you want a string of complaints. You can come out when you've had plenty."

"How many complaints are plenty, Mrs Jane?"

96   Emily Sarah Holt

"One," said Mrs Jane, marching off. "Plenty for me."

Rhoda lifted the latch, and walked in, Phoebe following her. She tapped at the inner door.

"Oh, come in, whoever it is," said a querulous, plaintive voice. "Well, Mrs Rhoda, I thought you would have been to see me before. A poor lonely creature, that nobody cares for, and never has any comfort nor pleasure! And who have you with you? I'm sure she's in a deep consumption from the looks of her. Coltsfoot, my dear, and horehound, with plenty of sugar, boiled together; and a little mallow won't hurt. But they'll not do you much good, I should say; you're too far gone: still, 'tis a duty to do all one can, and some strange things do happen: like Betty Collins—the doctors all gave her up, and there she is, walking about, as well as anybody. And so may you, my dear, though you don't look like it. Still, you are young—there's no telling: and coltsfoot is a very good thing, and makes wonderful cures. Oh, that careless Jane, to leave me all alone, just when I wanted my pillows shaking! And so inconsiderate of Nell to go home just to-day, of all days, when she knew I was sure to be worse; I always am after a fast-day. Fast-days don't suit me at all; they are very bad for sick people. They make one's spirits so low, and are sure to give me the vapours. Oh dear, that Jane!"

"What's the matter with that Jane?" demanded the bearer of the name, stalking in, as Phoebe was trying to brace up her courage to the point of offering to shake the pillows. "Want another dose of castor oil? I've got it."

A faint shriek of deprecation was the answer.

"Oh dear! And you know how I hate it! Jane, do shake up my pillows. They feel as if there were stones instead of flocks in them, or—"

"Nutmegs, no doubt," suggested Mrs Jane. "Shake them up? Oh yes, and you too—do you both good."

"Oh, don't, Jane! Have you an orange for me?"

"Sit down, my dears," said Mrs Jane, parenthetically. "Can't afford them, Marcella. Plenty of black currant tea. Better for you."

"I don't like it!" said Mrs Marcella, plaintively.

"Oranges are eightpence a-piece, and currants may be had for the gathering," observed Mrs Jane, sententiously.

"They give me a pain in my side!" moaned the invalid.

"Well, the oranges would give you a pain in your purse. I'd rather have one in my side, if I were you."

"You don't know what it is to be ill!" said Mrs Marcella, closing her eyes.

"Don't I? I've had both small-pox and spotted fever."

"So long ago!"

"Bless you, child! I'm not Methuselah!" said Mrs Jane.

"Well, I think you might be, Jane, for really, the way in which you can sit up all night, and look as fresh as a daisy in the morning, when you have not had a wink of sleep, and I am perfectly worn-out with suffering—just skin and bone, and no more—"

Emily Sarah Holt

"There's a little tongue left, I reckon!" said Mrs Jane.

"The way she will get up and go to market, my dears, after such a night as that," pursued Mrs Marcella, who always ran on her own line of rails, and never shunted to avoid collision; "you never saw anything like her—the amount she can bear! She's as tough as a rhinoceros, and as strong as an elephant, and as wanting in feeling as—as—"

"A sensitive plant," popped in Mrs Jane. "Now, Marcella, open your mouth and shut your eyes, and take this."

"Is it castor oil?" faintly screamed the invalid, endeavouring to protect herself.

"Stuff! 'Tis good Tent wine. Take it and be thankful."

"Where did you get it, Jane?"

"Ask me no questions, and I'll tell you no lies," said Mrs Jane. "It was honestly come by."

"Well, I think we must be going, Mrs Marcella," said Rhoda, rising.

"Oh, my dear! Must you, really? And so seldom as you come to see a poor thing like me, who hasn't a living creature to care for her—except Jane, of course, and she doesn't, not one bit! Dear! And to think that I was once a pretty young maid, with a little fortune of my own; and there was many a young gentleman, my dear, that would have given his right hand for no more than a smile from me—"

"Heyday! how this world is given to lying!" interpolated Mrs Jane.

"And we were a large family then—eight of us, my dear; and now they are all dead, and I am left quite alone, except Jane, you know. Oh dear, dear, but to think of it! But there is no thankfulness in the world, nor kindness neither. The people I have been good to! and now that I have *come down* a little, to see how they treat me! Jane doesn't mind it; she has no tender feelings at all; she can stand all things, and never say a word, I am sure I don't know how she does it. I am all feeling! These things touch me so keenly. But Jane's just like a stone. Well, good evening, my dear, if you must go. I think you might have come a little sooner, and you might come oftener, if you would. But that is always my lot, to be neglected and despised—a poor, lonely, ugly old maid, that nobody cares for. And it wasn't my fault, I am sure; I never chose such a fate. I cannot think why such afflictions have been sent me. I am sure I am no worse than other people. Clarissa is a great deal vainer than I am; and Jane is ever so much harder; and as to Dorothy, why, 'tis misery to see her— she is so cheerful and full of mirth, and she has not a thing to be content with—it quite hurts me to see anyone like that. But people are so wanting in feeling! I am sure—"

"Go, if you want," said Mrs Jane, shortly, holding the door open.

"Oh, yes, go! Of course you want to go!" lamented Mrs Marcella. "What pleasure can there be to a bright young maid like you, to sit with a poor, sick, miserable creature like me? Dear, dear! And only to think—"

Rhoda escaped. Phoebe followed, more slowly. Mrs Jane came out after them, and shut the door behind them.

"She's in pain, this evening," said the last-named person in her usual blunt style. "Some folks can bear pain, and some can't. And those that can must beat with those that can't.

Emily Sarah Holt

She'll be better of letting it out a bit. Good evening."

"Oh, isn't it dreadful!" said Rhoda, when they were out of the gate. "I just hate going to see Mrs Marcella, especially when she takes one of her complaining fits. If I were Mrs Jane, I should let her have it out by herself. But she is hard, rather—she doesn't care as I should."

But Phoebe thought that a mistake. She had noticed the drawn brow of the silent sister, while the sufferer was detailing her string of troubles, and the sudden quiver of the under lip, when allusion was made to the eight of whom the family had once consisted: and Phoebe's deduction was, not that Jane Talbot bore no burden, but that she kept it out of sight. Perhaps that very characteristic bluntness of her manner denoted a tight curb kept upon her spirit.

Rhoda had noticed nothing of all this. Herself a surface character, she could not see below the surface in another.

The Wednesday evening came, and with it Sir Richard Delawarr's coach, conveying his two younger daughters. They were extremely unlike in person. Gatty was tall, calm, and deliberate; Molly was rather diminutive for her years, and exceedingly lively. While Gatty came forward in a stately, courteous manner, courtesying to Madam, and kindly answering her inquiries after Betty, Molly linked her arm in Rhoda's, with—

"How goes it, old jade?"

And when Mr Onslow, who happened to be crossing the hall, stopped and inquired in a rather timid manner if Mrs Betty's health were improving, Molly at once favoured him with a slap on the back, and the counter query,—

"What's that to you, you old thief?" Phoebe was horrified. If these were aristocratic manners, she preferred those of inferior quality. But noticing that Gatty's manners were quiet and correct, Phoebe concluded that Molly must be an exceptional eccentricity. She contemplated the prospect of a month in that young lady's company with unmitigated repugnance.

"Well, Mrs Molly, my dear,—as smart as ever!" remarked Madam, turning to Molly with a smile. "All right, old witch!" said Molly. And to Phoebe's astonishment, Madam smiled on, and did not resent the impertinence.

"Well!—how do you like Gatty and Molly?" said Rhoda to Phoebe, when they were safe in their own room.

"Pretty well, Mrs Gatty," replied Phoebe, leaving the question of Molly undecided.

"Don't you like Molly?" demanded Rhoda, laughing. "Ah! I see. She's rather too clever to please you."

"I ask your pardon, but I don't see any cleverness in down-right rudeness," timidly suggested Phoebe.

"Oh, nobody cares what Molly says," answered Rhoda. "They put up with all that,—she's so smart. You see, she's very, very ingenious, and everybody thinks so, and she knows people think so. She's a rep., you see, and she has to keep it up."

"I ask your pardon," said Phoebe again; "a *what*, if you please?"

"A rep., child," answered Rhoda, in her patronising style. "A reputation,—a character for smartness, you know. Don't you see?"

"Well, I would rather have a character for something better," said Phoebe.

"You may make yourself easy; you'll never get a character for smartness," responded her cousin with an unpleasant laugh. "Well, I say, Phoebe, while they are here I shall have Molly in my room, and you must sleep with Gatty. You can come in and dress me of a morning, you know, and help me into bed at night; but we can't do with three in one room."

Phoebe was inwardly thankful for it. What little she had seen of Gatty was rather negative than positive; but at least it had not, as in the case of Molly revealed anything actively disagreeable. Rhoda was heartily welcome to Molly's society so far as Phoebe was concerned. But it surprised and rather perplexed Phoebe to find that Rhoda actually liked this very objectionable maiden.

"Panem?" asked Molly, the next morning at breakfast. Her Latin, such as it was, was entirely unburdened with cases and declensions. "Thank you, I will take kakos."

"Fiddle-de-dee! what's that?" said Molly. Rhoda had completely forgotten what the word meant.

"Oh, 'tis the Greek for biscuit," said she, daringly.

Phoebe contrived to hide a portion of her face in her teacup, but Gatty saw her eyes, and read their meaning.

"The Greek!" cried Molly. "Who has taught you Greek, Ne'er-do-well?"

"A very learned person," said Rhoda, to whom it was delight to mystify Molly.

"Old Onslow?" demanded irreverent Molly, quite undeterred by the consideration that the chaplain sat at the table with her.

"You can ask him," said Rhoda.

"Did you, old cassock?" inquired Molly, who appeared to apply that adjective in a most impartial manner.

"Indeed, Mrs Molly, I did not—I never knew—" stammered the startled chaplain, quite shaken out of his propriety.

"Never knew any Greek? I thought so," responded audacious Molly, thereby evoking laughter all round the table, in which even Madam joined.

Phoebe, who had recovered herself, sat lost in wonder where the cleverness of all this was to be found. It simply disgusted her. Rhoda was not always pleasant to put up with, but Rhoda was sweetness and grace, compared with Molly. Gatty sat quietly, neither rebuking her sister's sallies, nor apparently amused by them. And Rhoda *liked* this girl! It was a mystery to Phoebe.

When night came Phoebe found her belongings transferred to Gatty's room. She assisted Rhoda to undress, herself silent, but a perpetual chatter being kept up between Rhoda and Molly on subjects not by any means interesting to Phoebe.

The latter was at length dismissed, and, with a sense of relief, she went slowly along the passage to the room in which she and Gatty were to sleep.

Though it was getting very late, the clock being on the stroke of ten, yet Gatty was not in bed. She seemed to have half undressed herself, and then to have thrown a scarf over her shoulders and sat down by the window. It was a beautiful night, and a flood of silvery moonlight threw the trees into deep shadow and lit up the open spaces almost like day. Phoebe came and stood at the window beside Gatty. Perhaps each was a little shy of the other; for some seconds passed in silence, and Phoebe was the first to speak.

"You like it," she said timidly.

"Oh, yes. 'Tis so quiet," was Gatty's answer.

Phoebe was thinking what she should say next, when Gatty rose, took off her scarf, which she folded neatly and put away in the wardrobe, finished her undressing, and got into bed, without another word beyond "Good-night."

For three weeks of the month which the visit was to last this proved to be the usual state of matters. Gatty and Phoebe regularly exchanged greetings, night and morning; but beyond this their conversation was limited to remarks upon the weather, and an occasional request that Phoebe would inspect the neat and proper condition of some part of Gatty's dress which she could not conveniently see. And Phoebe began to come to the conclusion that Rhoda had judged rightly,—Gatty had nothing in her.

But one evening, when Molly had been surpassingly "clever," keeping Rhoda in peals of laughter, and Phoebe in a state of annoyed disgust,—on reaching their bedroom, Phoebe found Gatty, still dressed, and sitting by the bed, with her face bowed upon her hands.

"I ask your pardon, but are you not well?" said Phoebe, in a sympathising tone.

"Oh, yes. Quite well," was Gatty's reply, in a constrained voice; but as she rose and moved her hands from her face, Phoebe saw that she had been crying.

"You are in trouble," said Phoebe, gently. "Don't tell me anything, unless you like; but I know what trouble is; and if I could help you—"

"You can't," said Gatty, shortly.

Phoebe was silent. Her sympathy had been repulsed—it was not wanted. The undressing was, as usual, without a word.

But when the girls had lain down in bed, Phoebe was a little surprised to hear Gatty say suddenly,—

"Phoebe Latrobe!—does anybody love you?"

"God loves me," said Phoebe, simply. "I am not sure that any one else does."

"I like you," said Gatty. "You let me be. That's what nobody ever does."

"I am not sure that I understand you," responded Phoebe.

"I'll tell you," replied Gatty, "for I think you can hold your tongue, and not be always chatter, chatter, chatter, like—like some people. You think there's only one Gatty Delawarr; and I'll be bound you think her a very dull, stupid creature. Well, you're about right there. But there are two: there's me, and there's the thing people want to make me. Now, you haven't seen me,—you've only seen the woman into whom I am being pinched and pulled. This is me that talks to you to-night, and perhaps you'll never see me again,—only that other girl,—so you had better make the most of me now that you have me. I'm sure, if you dislike her as much as I do—! You see, Phoebe, there are three of us—Betty, and me, and Molly: and Mother's set her heart on our all making a noise in the world. Well, perhaps we could have managed better if we might have made our own noise; but we have to make it to order, and we don't do it well at all. Betty's the best off, because Mother hit on something that went with her nature,—she's the notable housewife. So she plays her play well. But when she set up Molly for a wit, and me for a beauty, she made a great blunder. Molly hasn't a bit of wit, so she falls back on rude speeches, and they go through me just as if she ran a knife into me. You did not think so, did you?"

"No," said Phoebe, wonderingly; "I thought you did not seem to care."

"That's the other Gatty. She does not care. She's been told,— oh, a hundred times over!—to compose herself and keep her features calm, and not let her voice be ruffled; and move slowly, so that her elbows are not square, and all on in that way; and she has about learned it by this time. I know how to sit still and look unconcerned, if my heart be breaking. And it is breaking, Phoebe."

"Dear Mrs Gatty, what can I do for you?"

"You can't do anything but listen to me. Let me pour it out this once, and don't scold me. I don't mean anything wrong, Phoebe. I don't wish to complain of Mother, or Molly, or any one. I only want to tell somebody what I have to bear, and then I'll compose myself again to my part in the world's big theatre, and go away and bear it, like other girls do. And you are the only person I have acquaintance with, that I feel as if I could tell."

"Pray go on, Mrs Gatty; I can feel sorry, if I can do nothing else."

"Well,—at home somebody is at me from morning to night. There's a posture-master comes once a week; and Mother's maid looks to my carriage at all times, 'tis an endless round of—'Gatty, hold your head up,'—'Gatty, put that plate down, and take it up with your arm rounded,'—'Gatty, you must not laugh,'—'Gatty, you must not sneeze,'—'Gatty, walk slower,'—come, that's enough. Then there's Molly on the top of it. And there's Betty on the top of Molly,—who can't conceive why anybody should ruffle her mind about any-thing. And there's Mother above all, for ever telling me she looks to have me cut a dash, and make a good match; and if I had played my cards rightly I ought to have caught a husband ere I was seventeen,—'tis disgraceful that I should thus throw away my advantages. And, Phoebe, *I* want nothing but to creep into some little, far-away corner, and *be me*, and throw away my patches and love-locks, and powder and pomatum, and never see that other Gatty any more. That's how it was up to last month."

Gatty paused a moment, and drew a long sigh.

"And then, there came another on the scene, and I suppose the play grew more entertaining to Mother, and Betty, and Molly, in the boxes. People don't think, you know, when they look down at the prima donna, painted, and smiling, and decked with flowers,—they don't think if she has a husband who ill-uses her, or a child dying at home. She has come there to make them sport. Well, there came an old lord,—a man of sixty or seventy,—who has led a wild rakish life all these years, and now he thinks 'tis time to settle down, and he wants me to help him to make people think he's become respectable. And they say I shall marry him. Phoebe, they say I must,—there is to be no help for it. And I can't bear

Emily Sarah Holt

him to look at me. If he touches my glove, I want to fling it into the fire when it comes off. And this one month, here, at White-Ladies, is my last quiet time. When I go home—if Betty be recovered of her distemper—I am to be married to this old man in a week's time. I am tied hand and foot, like a captive or a slave; and I have not even the poor relief of tears. They make my eyes red, and I must not make, my eyes red, if it would save my life. But nothing will save me. The lambs that used to be led to the altar are not more helpless than I. The rope is round my neck; and I must trot on beside the executioner, and find what comfort I can in the garland of roses on my head."

There was a silence of a few seconds after Gatty finished her miserable tale. And then Phoebe's voice asked softly,—

"Dear Mrs Gatty, have you asked God to save you?"

"What's the use?" answered Gatty, in a hopeless tone.

"Because He would do it," said Phoebe. "I don't know how. It might be by changing my Lady Delawarr's mind, or the old lord's, or yours; or many another way; I don't know how. But I do know that He has promised to bring no temptation on those that fear Him, beyond what they shall be able to bear."

"Oh, I don't know!" said Gatty, in that tone which makes the word sound like a cry of pain.

"Have you tried entreating my Lady Delawarr?"

"Tried! I should think so. And what do you think I get by it? 'Gatty, my dear, 'tis so unmodish to be thus warm over anything! Compose yourself, and control your feelings. Love!—no, of course you do not love my Lord Polesworth, while you are yet a maid; 'twould be highly indecorous for you to do any such thing. But when you are his wife, you'll be perfectly content; and that is all you can expect. My dear, do compose yourself, or your face will be quite wrinkled; and let me hear no more of this nonsense, I beg of you. Maids cannot look to choose for themselves, 'tis not reasonable.' That is what I get, Phoebe."

"And your father, Mrs Gatty?"

"My father? Oh! 'Really, Gatty, I can't interfere,—'tis your mother's affair; you must make up your mind to it. We can't have always what we like,'—and then he whistles to his hounds, and goes out a-hunting."

"Well, Mrs Gatty, suppose you try God?"

"Suppose I have done, Phoebe, and got no answer at all?"

"Forgive me, I cannot suppose it."

"Is He so good to *you*, Phoebe?"

The question was asked in a very, very mournful tone.

"Mrs Gatty," said Phoebe, softly, "He has given me Himself. I do not think He has given me anything else of what my heart longs for. But that is enough. In Him I have all things."

"What do you mean?" came in accents of perplexity from the bed in the opposite corner.

"I am afraid," said Phoebe, "I cannot tell you. I mean, I could not make you understand it."

"'Given you Himself!'" repeated Gatty. "I can fancy how He could reward you or make you happy; but, 'give

Emily Sarah Holt

you Himself!'"

"Well, I cannot explain it," said Phoebe. "Yes, it means giving happiness; but it means a great deal more. I can feel it, but I cannot put it in words."

"I don't understand you the least bit!"

"Will you talk awhile with Mrs Dolly Jennings, and see if she can explain it to you? I do not think any one can, in words; but I guess she would come nearer to it than I could."

"I like Mrs Dolly," said Gatty, thoughtfully; "she is very kind."

"Very," assented Phoebe.

"I think I should not mind talking to her," said Gatty. "We will walk down there to-morrow, if we can get leave."

"And now, had we not better go to sleep?" suggested Phoebe.

"Well, we can try," sighed Gatty. "But, Phoebe, 'tis no good telling me to pray, because I have done it. I said over every collect in the Prayer-book—ten a day; and the very morning after I had finished them, that horrid man came, and Mother made—I had to go down and sit half an hour listening to him. Praying does no good."

"I am not sure that you have tried it," said Phoebe.

"Didn't I tell you, this minute, I said every—"

"I ask your pardon for interrupting you, but saying is not praying. Did you really pray them?"

"Phoebe, I do not understand you! How could I pray them and not say them?"

"Well, I did not quite mean that," said Phoebe; "but please, Mrs Gatty, did you feel them? Did you really ask God all the collects say, or did you only repeat the words over? You see, if I felt cold in bed, I might ask Mrs Betty to give me leave to have another blanket; but if I only kept saying that I was cold, to myself, over and over, and did not tell Mrs Betty, I should be long enough before I got the blanket. Did you say the collects to yourself, Mrs Gatty, or did you say them to the Lord?"

There was a pause before Gatty said, in rather an awed voice, "Phoebe, when you pray, is God there?"

"Yes," said Phoebe, readily.

"He is not, with me," replied Gatty. "He feels a long, long way off; and I feel as if my collects might drop and be lost before they can get up to Him. Don't you?"

"Never," answered Phoebe. "But I don't send my prayers up by themselves; I give them to Jesus Christ to carry. He never drops one, Mrs Gatty."

"'Tis all something I don't understand one bit," said Gatty, wearily. "Go to sleep, Phoebe; I won't keep you awake. But we'll go and see Mrs Dolly."

The next afternoon, when Rhoda and Molly had disappeared on their private affairs, Gatty dropped a courtesy to Madam, and requested her permission to visit Mrs Dolly Jennings.

"By all means, my dear," answered Madam, affably. "If Rhoda has no occasion for her, let Phoebe wait on you."

The second request which had been on Gatty's lips being thus forestalled, the girls set forth—without consulting Rhoda, which Gatty was disinclined to do, and which Phoebe fancied that she had done—and reached the Maidens' Lodge without falling in with any disturbing element, such as either Rhoda or Molly would unquestionably have been. Mrs Dorothy received them in her usual kindly manner, and gave them tea before they entered on the subject of which both the young minds were full. Then Gatty told her story, if very much the same terms as she had given it to Phoebe.

"And I can't understand Phoebe, Mrs Dolly," she ended. "She says God has given her Himself; and I cannot make it out. And she says she gives her prayers to Jesus Christ to carry. I don't know what she means. It sounds good. But I don't understand it—not one bit."

Mrs Dorothy came up to where Gatty was sitting, and took the girl's head between her small, thin hands. It was not a beautiful face; but it was pleasant enough to look on, and would have been more so, but for the discipline which had crushed out of it all natural interest and youthful anticipation, and had left that strange, strained look of care and forced calm upon the white brow.

"Dear child," she said, gently, "you want rest, don't you?"

Gatty's grey eyes filled with tears.

"That is just what I do want, Mrs Dolly," she said, "somewhere where I could be quiet, and be let alone, and just be myself and not somebody else."

"Ah, my dear!" said Mrs Dorothy, shaking her head, "you never get let alone in this world. Satan won't let you alone, if men do. But to be yourself—that is what God wants of you.

At least 'tis one half of what He would have; the other half is that you should give yourself to Him."

"'Tis no good praying," said Gatty, as before.

"Did the Lord tell you that, my dear?"

"No!" said Gatty, looking up in surprise.

"Well, I would not say it till He does, child. But what did you pray for?"

"I said all the collects over."

"Very good things, my dear; but were they what you wanted? I thought you had a special trouble at this time."

"But what could I do?" asked Gatty, apparently rather bewildered.

"Dear child, thou couldst sure ask thy Father to help thee, without more ado. But 'bide a wee,' as my old friend, Scots Davie, was wont to say. There is a great deal about prayer in the Word of God. Let us look at a little of it." Little Mrs Dorothy trotted to her small work-table, which generally stood at her side, and came back with a well-worn brown Bible. Gatty watched her with a rather frightened look, as if she thought that something was going to be done to her, and was not sure whether it might hurt her.

"Now hearken: 'Be careful for nothing; but in everything, by prayer and supplication, with thanksgiving, let your requests be made known unto God.' Again: 'Whatsoever ye shall ask in My Name, that will I do.' These are grand words, my dear."

"But they can't mean that Mrs Dorothy! Why, only think—if I were to ask for a fortune, should I get it?"

"I must have two questions answered, my dear, ere I can tell that. Who are the *you* in these verses?"

"I thought it meant everybody."

"Not so. Listen again: 'If ye abide in Me, and My words abide in you, ye shall ask what ye will, and it shall be done unto you.' 'Tis not everybody doth that."

"But I don't know what that means, Mrs Dorothy."

"Then, my dear, you have answered my second question— Are you one of these? For if you know not even what the thing is, 'tis but reasonable to conclude you have never known it in your own person."

"I suppose not," said Gatty, sorrowfully.

"You see, my dear, 'tis to certain persons these words are said. If you are not one of these persons, then they are not said to you."

"I am not." And Gatty shook her head sadly. "But, Mrs Dorothy, what does it mean?"

"Dear," said the old lady, "when we do truly abide in Christ, we desire first of all that His will be done. We wish for this or that; but we wish more than all that He choose all things for us—that He have His own way. Our wills are become His will. It follows as a certainty, that they shall be done. We must have what we wish, when it is what He wishes who rules all things. 'Ye shall ask what ye will.' He guides us what to ask, if we beg Him to do so."

"Is any one thus much perfect?" inquired Gatty, doubtfully.

"Many are trying for it," said Mrs Dolly. "There may be but few that have fully reached it."

"But that makes us like machines, Mrs Dolly, moved about at another's will."

"What, my dear! Love makes us machines? Never! The very last thing that could be, child."

"I don't know much about love," said Gatty, drearily.

"About love, or about being loved?" responded Mrs Dolly.

"Both," answered the girl, in the same tone.

"Will you try it, my dear? 'Tis the sweetener of all human life."

Gatty looked up with a surprised expression.

"*I* can't make people love me," she said.

"Nor can you make yourself love others," added Mrs Dorothy. "But you can ask the Lord for that fairest of all His gifts, saving Jesus Christ."

"Ask God for a beau! O Mrs Dorothy!" exclaimed Gatty in a shocked tone.

"My dear, I never so much as named one," responded Mrs Dorothy, with a little laugh. "Sure, you are not one of those foolish maids that think they must be loveless and forlorn without they have a husband?"

Gatty had always been taught to think so; and she looked bewildered and mystified. A more eligible husband than old Lord Polesworth was the only idea that associated itself in her mind with the word love.

"But what else did you mean?" she asked.

"Ay me!" said Mrs Dorothy, as if to herself. "How do men misunderstand God! Child, wert thou never taught the first and great commandment? 'Thou shalt love the Lord thy God with all thine heart, and with all thy mind, and with all thy soul, and with all thy strength?'"

"Oh, of course," said Gatty, as if she were listening to some scientific formula about a matter wherein she was not at all concerned.

"Have you done that, my dear?"

"Done what?" demanded Gatty in a startled tone.

"Have you loved God with all your heart?"

Gatty looked as if she had been suddenly roused from sleep, and was unable to take in the circumstances.

"I don't know! I—I suppose, so."

"You suppose so! Dear child, how can you love any, and not know it?"

"But that is quite another sort of love!" cried Gatty.

"There is no sort but one, my dear. Love is love."

"Oh, but we can't *love* God!" said Gatty, as if the idea quite shocked her. "That means—it means reverence, you know, and duty, and so on. It can't mean anything else, Mrs Dorothy."

Mrs Dorothy knitted very fast for a moment. Phoebe saw that her eyes were filled with tears.

"Poor lost sheep!" she said, in a grieved voice. "Poor straying lamb, whom the wolf hath taught to be frightened of the Shepherd! You did not find that in the Bible, my dear."

"Oh, but words don't mean the same in the Bible!" urged Gatty. "Surely, Mrs Dorothy, 'twould be quite unreverent to think so."

"Surely, my dear, it were more unreverent to think that God does not mean what He saith. When He saith, 'I will punish you seven times for your sins,' He means it, Mrs Gatty. And when He saith, 'I will be a Father unto you,' shall we say He doth not mean it? O my dear, don't do Him such an injury as that!"

"Do God an injury!" said Gatty in an awed whisper.

"Ay, a cruel injury!" was the answer. "Men are always injuring God. Either they try to persuade themselves that He means not what He says when He threatens: or else they shut their hearts up close, and then fancy that His heart is shut up too. My dear, He did not tarry to offer to be your Father, until you came and asked Him for it. 'He *first* loved you.' Child, what dost thou know of the Lord Jesus Christ?"

Ah, what did she know? For Gatty lived in a dreary time, when religion was at one of its lowest ebb-tides, and had sunk almost to the level of heathen morality. If Gatty had been required to give definitions of the greatest words in the

Emily Sarah Holt

language, and had really done it from the bottom of her heart, according to her own honest belief, the list would have run much in this way:—

"God.—The Great First Cause of all things, who has nothing to do with anything now, but will, at some remote period, punish murderers, thieves, and very wicked people."

"Christ.—A supernaturally good man, who was crucified seventeen hundred years ago."

"Heaven.—A delightful place, where everybody is happy, to which all respectable people will go, when they can't help it any longer."

"Bible.—A good book read in church; intensely dry, as good books always are no concern of mine."

"Salvation, peace, holiness, and the like.—Words in the Prayer-Book."

"Faith, hope, love, etcetera.—Duties, which of course we all perform, and therefore don't need to trouble ourselves about them."

"Prayer.—An incantation, to be repeated morning and evening, if you wish to avert ill luck during the day."

These were Gatty's views—if she could be said to have any. How different from those of Mrs Dorothy Jennings! To her, God was the Creator, from whom, and by whom, and to whom, were all things: the Fountain of Mercy, who had so loved the world as to give His only-begotten Son for its salvation: the Father who, having loved her before the world was, cared for everything, however insignificant, which concerned her welfare. Christ was the Friend who sticketh closer than a brother—the Lamb who had been slain for her, the High Priest who was touched with every feeling of human infirmity. Heaven was the home which her Father had prepared for her. The Bible was the means whereby her Father talked with her; and prayer the means whereby she talked with Him. Salvation was her condition; holiness, her aim; faith, love, peace, the very breath she drew. While, in Gatty's eyes, all this was unknown and unreal, to Mrs Dorothy it was the most real thing in all the world.

Gatty answered her friend's query by a puzzled look.

"It comes in church," she said. "He is in the Creed, and at the end of the prayers. I don't know!"

"Child," replied Mrs Dorothy, "you don't know Him. And, Mrs Gatty, my dear, you must know Him, if you are ever to be a happy woman. O poor child, poor child! To think that the Man who loved you and gave His life for you is no more to you than one of a row of figures, a name set to the end of a prayer!"

Gatty was taken by surprise. She looked up with both unwonted emotion and astonishment in her eyes.

"Mrs Dolly," she said, with feeling, "I cannot tell, but I think 'twould be pleasant to feel like you. It sounds all real, as if you had a live friend."

"That is just what it is, my dear Mrs Gatty. A Friend that loves me enough to count the very hairs of my head,—to whom nothing is a little matter that can concern me. And He is just as ready to be your Friend too."

"What makes you think so, Mrs Dolly?"

"My dear, He died on purpose to save you."

"The world, not me!" said Gatty.

"If there had been no world but you," was the answer, "He would have thought it worth while."

Gatty's answer was not immediate. When it came, it was—

"What does He want me to do?"

"He wants you to give Him your heart," said the old lady. "Do that first, and you will very soon find out how to give Him your hands and your head."

"And will He keep away my Lord Polesworth?" asked the girl, earnestly.

"He will keep away everything that can hurt you. Not, maybe, everything you don't like. Sometimes 'tis just the contrary. The sweet cake that you like might harm you, and the physic you hate might heal you. If so, He will give you the physic. But, child, if you are His own, He will put the cup into your had with a smite which will make it easy to take."

"I should like that," said Gatty, wistfully. "But could it be right to wed with my Lord Polesworth, when I could not love nor honour him in my heart at all?"

"It can never be right to lie. Ask God to make you a way of escape, if so it be."

"What way?"

"Leave that to Him."

Mrs Dorothy's little clock struck four.

"I think, if you please, Mrs Gatty," said Phoebe's hitherto silent voice, "that Madam will be looking for us."

"Yes, I guess she will," answered Gatty, rising, and courtesying. "I thank you, Mrs Dolly. You have given me a ray of hope—if 'twill not die away."

Mrs Dorothy drew the girl to her, and kissed her cheek.

"Christ cannot die, my child," she replied. "And Christ's love is deathless as Himself. 'Death hath no more dominion over Him.' And He saith to His own, 'Because I live, ye shall live also.'"

"It should be a better life than this," said Gatty, with a sigh.

"This is not the Christian's life, my dear. 'His life is hid with Christ in God.' 'Tis not left in his own hands to keep; he would soon lose it, if it were. Farewell, dear child; and may the Lord keep thee!"

Gatty looked up suddenly. "Tell me what to say to Him."

Mrs Dorothy scarcely hesitated a moment.

"'Teach me to do Thy will,'" she answered. "That holds everything. You cannot do His will unless you are one of His redeemed. He must save you, and hold you up, and guide you to glory, if you do His will—not because you do it, for the salvation cometh first; but without the one, there cannot be the other. And he that doeth the will of God soon learns to love it, better than any mortal thing. 'Oh, how love I Thy law!' saith David. 'There is nothing on earth that I desire in comparison of Thee.'"

She kissed both the girls again, and they went away.

CHAPTER SIX

TRAPS LAID FOR RHODA

"La souveraine habilite consiste a bien connoitre le prix des choses."

La Rochefoucauld.

There was an earnest, wistful, far-away look in Gatty's eyes, as though some treasure-house had been opened to her, the existence of which she had never previously suspected; but neither she nor Phoebe said a word to each other as they crossed the Park, and went up the wide white steps of the Abbey.

"Where on earth have you been, you gadabouts?" came in Rhoda's voice from the interior of the hall. "Oh, but I've such a jolly piece of news for you! Molly and me heard it from Madam. Guess what it is."

Rhoda's grammar was more free and easy than correct at all times; and Phoebe could not help thinking that in that respect, as in others, she had perceptibly deteriorated by contact with Molly.

"I don't care to hear it, thank you," said Gatty, rather hastily,

Emily Sarah Holt

walking straight upstairs.

"Oh, don't you, Mrs Prim?" demanded Rhoda. "Well, it doesn't concern you much. Now, Phoebe, guess!"

Phoebe felt very little in tune for the sort of amusement usually patronised by Rhoda. But she set herself to gratify that rather exacting young lady.

"I don't guess things well," she said. "Is one of your aunts coming?"

"My aunts!" repeated Rhoda, in supreme scorn. "Not if I know it, thank you. I said it was jolly. Why, Phoebe! to guess such a thing as that!"

"Well, I should be pleased enough if mine were coming to see me," said Phoebe, good-temperedly. "I don't know what else to guess. Has some one given you a present?"

"Wish they had!" ejaculated Rhoda. "No, I'm sorry to say nobody's had so much good sense. But there's somebody—I shall have to tell you sooner or later, you stupid goose, so I may as well do it now—somebody's coming to Number Four. Mrs Eleanor Darcy, a cousin of my Lord Polesworth—only think!—and (that's best of all) she's got a nephew."

"How is that best of all?" asked Phoebe.

"Mr Marcus Welles—isn't it a pretty name?—and he will come with her, to settle her in her new house. '*Why?*' Oh, what a silly Phoebe you are! He has three thousand a year."

"Then I should think he might take better care of his aunt than let her be an indigent gentlewoman," said Phoebe, rather warmly.

"As if he would want to be pothered with an old aunt!" cried Rhoda. "But I'll tell you what (you are so silly, you want telling everything!)—I mean to set my cap at him."

"Won't you have some cleaner lace on it first?" suggested Phoebe, with the exceedingly quiet, dry fun which was one of her characteristics.

"You stupid, literal thing!" said Rhoda. "I might as well talk to the cat. Oh, here you come, Molly! Now for tea, if 'tis ready, and then—"

Madam was already at the tea-table, and Baxter was just bringing in the kettle.

"I trust you have had a pleasant walk, my dears," said she, kindly, as the four girls filed in—Molly first, Phoebe last.

"Middling," said Molly, taking the initiative as usual. "Robbed seventeen birds' nests, climbed twenty-four trees, and jumped over a dozen five-barred gates."

"Oh, did you!" murmured Phoebe, in a shocked tone, too horrified for silence.

Rhoda went into convulsions behind her handkerchief.

"Innocent little darling!" exclaimed Molly; "she thinks we did!"

"You said so," answered Phoebe, reproachfully.

"You are so smart, my dear Mrs Molly," said Madam, smilingly. "Did you all walk together?"

"No, I thank you!" responded Molly. "Gatty and the innocent

Emily Sarah Holt

little dear went to a Quakers' meeting."

Had Madam taken the assertion literally, she would have been alarmed and horrified indeed; for at that time all Dissenters were considered dangerous characters, and Quakers the worst of all. But, recognising it as one of Molly's flights of intellect, she smiled placidly, and said no more.

"My dear, I think you will be acquainted with Mrs Eleanor Darcy?" asked Madam, addressing herself to Gatty.

"She has visited my mother, but only once," answered Gatty.

"Oh, the pootsy-bootsy!" broke in Molly. "Isn't she a sweet, charming, handsome creature?—the precious dear!"

"I fear she doth not please you, Mrs Molly?" asked Madam, interpreting Molly's exclamation by the rule of contrary.

"She's the ugliest old baboon that ever grinned!" was Molly's complimentary reply.

"What say you, Mrs Gatty?"

"She is certainly not handsome," answered Gatty, apparently with some reluctance; "but I have heard her well spoken of, as very kind and good."

"Have you met with Mr Welles, her nephew, my dear?"

Molly had clasped her hands, leaned back, lifted her eyes with an expression of sentimental rapture, and was executing an effective *tableau vivant*.

"Yes, I have seen him two or three times," said Gatty.

"Is he a young man of an agreeable turn?" inquired Madam.

"He is very handsome," replied Gatty, rather doubtfully, as if she hardly knew what to say.

"Pleasant as a companion?" pursued Madam.

"People generally think so, I believe," answered Gatty, with studied vagueness.

"You dear old concatenation, you'll get nothing out of my wretch of a sister," impetuously cried Molly.

"I'll tell you all about Marcus. He's the brightest eyes that ever shone, and the sweetest voice that praised your fine eyes, and the most delightful manners! White hands, and a capital leg, and never treads on your corns. Oh, there's nobody like him. I mean to marry him."

"Molly!" said Gatty. It was the first time she had offered anything like a reproof to her sister.

"Now, you hold your tongue, Mrs Prude!" responded Molly. "You're not a bit better than I am."

Gatty made no reply.

"Don't you set up to be either a prig or a saint!" continued Molly, angrily. "Betty's enough. She isn't a saint; but she's a prig. If ever you're either, I'll lead you a life!"

And there could be little doubt of Molly's fulfilling her threat.

The next day, Gatty and Molly Delawarr went home. Betty had quite recovered, and was gone to stay with a friend near

Bristol; the house had been thoroughly disinfected, and was pronounced free from all danger; and Lady Delawarr thought there was no longer need for the girls to remain away.

"I wonder what will become of me without you, Molly!" said Rhoda, dolefully.

"Oh, you'll have plenty to do, old Gatepost," observed Molly, apparently in allusion to Rhoda's uneventful life. "You've got to fall in love with Marcus. I'll cut you into slices if you do, and make buttered toast of you."

"Good-bye!" said Rhoda laughing.

"*Vale!*" responded Molly.

"Good-bye, dear little Phoebe!" was Gatty's farewell. "I wonder what would have become of me if I had not met you and Mrs Dorothy. For I have asked Him to be my Friend,— you know,—and I think, I *think* He will."

"I am sure of it. Good-bye."

And so Gatty and Molly passed out of the life at White-Ladies.

On returning to the old order of things, Phoebe found Rhoda, as she expected, considerably changed for the worse. What had been a sort of good-humoured condescension was altered into absolute snappishness, and Phoebe was sorely tried. But the influence of Molly, bad as it had been, proved temporary. Rhoda sank by degrees—or shall I say rose?— into her old self, and Phoebe presently had no more to bear than before the visit from Delawarr Court.

About a fortnight after the departure of Gatty and Molly, as

Phoebe was sitting at the parlour window with her work, she perceived Mrs Jane Talbot, hooded, cloaked, and pattened,—for the afternoon was damp,—marching up to the side door. The fact was communicated to Madam, who rose and glanced at herself in the chimney-glass, and ringing her little hand-bell, desired Baxter to show Mrs Jane into the parlour.

"Good afternoon, Mrs Jane; 'tis a pleasure I did not look for," said Madam, as she rose.

"Your servant, Madam," returned Mrs Jane, who had divested herself of cloak and pattens in the hall.

"Pray be seated, Mrs Jane. And what brings you hither?—for methinks some matter of import will have called you out on so rainy a day as this."

"Easy to guess," answered Mrs Jane, taking a seat as requested, and delivering her communication in short, blunt sentences, like small shot. "A whim of Marcella's. Got a fancy for Port O Port. Sent me to beg a sup of you, Madam. Fancies it will cure her. Fiftieth time she has thought so, of something. All nonsense. Can't help it."

"Indeed, my dear Mrs Jane, I am happy to be capable of helping Mrs Marcella to her fancy, and trust it may be of the advantage she thinks.—Phoebe! tell Betty to bid Baxter bring hither a bottle of the best Port O Port—that from the little ark in the further cellar.—And how does Mrs Marcella this afternoon?"

"As cross as two sticks," said Mrs Jane.

"She is a great sufferer," observed Madam, in her kindest manner.

Emily Sarah Holt

Mrs Jane made no reply, unless her next remark could properly be called one.

"Mrs Darcy came last night."

"Last night!" answered Madam, in accents of surprise. "Dear! I quite understood she was not to arrive before this evening. You have seen her, Mrs Jane?"

"Seen her! Oh dear, yes; I've seen her. We were schoolfellows."

"Were you, indeed? That I did not know. 'Twill be a pleasure to you, Mrs Jane, to have an old schoolfellow so near."

"Depends," said Mrs Jane sententiously.

"No doubt," answered Madam. "Were you and Mrs Eleanor friends at school, Mrs Jane?"

"No, Madam."

"Not? Perhaps you were not near enough of an age."

"Only six months between. No; that wasn't it. I was a silly scapegrace, and she was a decent, good maid. Too good for me. I haven't got any better. And she hasn't got any handsomer."

"Pray forgive me," replied Madam, with a smile, "but I cannot think that name applies to you now, Mrs Jane. And was her nephew with Mrs Eleanor; as he engaged?"

"Large as life," said Mrs Jane.

"And how large is that, in his case?" inquired Madam.

"Asking him or me?" retorted Mrs Jane. "*I* should say, about as big as a field mouse. He thinks himself big enough to overtop all the elephants in creation. Marcus Welles! Oh, yes, I'll mark him well,—you trust me."

It was tolerably evident that Mr Welles had not succeeded in fascinating Mrs Jane, whatever he might do to other people.

"I was told he was extreme handsome?" remarked Madam, in a tone of inquiry.

Mrs Jane's exclamation in response sounded very like— "Pish!"

"You think not, Mrs Jane?"

"Folks' eyes are so different, Madam," answered Mrs Jane. "Chinamen's beauties wouldn't go for much in England, I guess. He's a silly, whimsical, finnicking piece—that's what he is! Pink velvet coat, laced with silver. Buff breeches. White silk stockings with silver clocks. No cloak. And raining cats and dogs and pitchforks. Reckon Eleanor got all the sense that was going in that family. None left for Mr Mark-me-well. Missed it, anyhow."

From that day forward, behind his back, Mark-me-well was the only name bestowed by Mrs Jane on the young man in question. To his face she gave him none,—an uncivil proceeding in 1714; but Mrs Jane being allowedly an eccentric character, no one expected her to conform to conventional rules on all occasions.

It would seem that Mr Welles wished to lose no time in paying his court to Madam; for that very evening, as soon as calling-hours began, he put in an appearance at White-Ladies.

Calling-hours and visiting-days were as common then as now; but the hours were not the same. From five to eight o'clock in the evening was the proper time for a visit of ceremony; candles were always lighted, there was a special form of knock, and the guests sat round the room in a prim circle.

Perhaps the "cats, dogs, and pitchforks" alluded to before had spoiled the pink and buff suit which had roused the scorn of Mrs Jane. The colours in which Mr Welles chose to make his *debut* at White-Ladies were violet and white. A violet velvet coat, trimmed with silver lace, was fastened with little silver hasps; white satin breeches led downwards to violet silk stockings with silver clocks, girt below the knee with silver garters. A three-cornered hat, of violet silk and silver lace, was heavily adorned with white plumes, and buttoned up at one side with a diamond. He wore shoes with silver buckles and very high red heels, white-silver fringed gloves, a small muff of violet velvet; and carried in his hand a slender amber-headed cane. Being a London beau of fashion, he was afflicted with a slight limp, and also with intense short-sightedness, which caused him to wear a gold eye-glass, constantly in use—except when alone, on which occasions Mr Welles became suddenly restored to the full use of his faculties.

He certainly was very handsome, and his taste was good. His wig was always suited to his complexion, and he rarely wore more than two colours, of which one was frequently black or white. Mr Welles was highly accomplished and highly fashionable; he played ombre and basset, the spinet and the violin; he sang and danced well, composed anagrams and acrostics, was a good rider, hunted fearlessly and gamed high, interlarded his conversation with puns, and was a thorough adept at small talk. He was personally acquainted with every actor on the London stage, and by sight with every politician in the Cabinet. His manners were of the new school then just rising—which means, that they were very free and easy, removed from all the minute and often cumbersome ceremonies which had distinguished the old school. He generally rose about noon, dined at three p.m., spent the evening at the opera or theatre, and went to bed towards morning. Add to this, that he collected old china, took much snuff, combed his wig in public, and was unable to write legibly or spell correctly—and a finished portrait is presented of Mr Marcus Welles, and through him of a fashionable London gentleman of his day.

The impression made by Mr Welles on the ladies at the Abbey was of varied character. Madam commended him, but with that faint praise which is nearly akin to censure. He was well favoured, she allowed, and seemed to be a man of parts; but in her young days it was considered courteous to lead a lady to a chair before a gentleman seated himself; and it was not considered courteous to omit the Madam in addressing her. Rhoda said very little in her grandmother's presence, reserving her opinion for Phoebe's private ear. But as soon as they were alone, the girls stated their ideas explicitly.

"Isn't he a love of a dear?" cried Rhoda, in ecstasy.

"No, I don't think he is," responded Phoebe, in a tone of unmistakable disgust.

"Why, Phoebe! Are you not sensible of the merit of such a man as that?"

"No, I am sure I did not see any," said Phoebe, as before.

"Oh, Phoebe! Such taste as he has! And his discourse! I never saw so quick a wit. I am sure he is a man of great reach, and a man of figure too. I shall think the time long till

I see him again."

"Dear me! I shan't!" exclaimed Phoebe. "Taste? Well, I suppose you may dress a doll with taste. His clothes are well enough, only they are too fine for anything but visiting."

"Well, wasn't he visiting, you silly Phoebe?"

"And he may be a man of figure—I don't know; but as to reach! I wonder what you saw in his discourse to admire; it seemed to me all about nothing."

"Why, that's just his parts!" said Rhoda. "Any man can talk about something; but to be able to talk in a clever, sprightly way about nothing—that takes a man of reach."

"Well! he may take his reach out of my reach," answered Phoebe, in a disgusted tone. "I shall think the time uncommonly short, I can promise you, till I see him again; for I never wish to do it."

"Phoebe, I do believe you haven't one bit of discernment!"

But Phoebe held her peace.

Madam called in due form on her new guest at the Maidens' Lodge, and Mrs Darcy returned the visit next day. She proved to be a short, stout, little woman, with a face which, while undeniably and excessively plain, was so beaming with good humour that it was difficult to remember her uncomeliness after the first *coup d'oeil*. Mr Welles accompanied her on the return visit. What had induced him to take up his quarters at the Bear, at Tewkesbury, was an enigma to the inhabitants of White-Ladies. Of course he could not live at the Maidens' Lodge, Madam being rigidly particular with respect to the intrusion of what Betty called "he creeturs" into that enchanted valley, and not tolerating the habitual presence even of a servant of the obnoxious sex. According to the representations of Mr Welles himself, he was fascinated by the converse and character of Madam, and was also completely devoted to his dear Aunt Eleanor. But Mr Welles had not favoured the Bear with very much of his attention before it dawned upon one person at least that neither Madam nor Mrs Eleanor had much to do with his frequent visits to Cressingham. Mrs Dorothy Jennings quickly noticed that Mr Welles was quite clever enough to discover what pleased different persons, and to adapt himself accordingly with surprising facility; and she soon perceived that the attraction was Rhoda, or rather Rhoda's prospects as the understood heiress of White-Ladies. Mr Welles accommodated himself skilfully to the prejudices of Madam; his manners assumed a graver and more courtly air, his conversation a calm and sensible tone; and Madam at length remarked to her grand-daughters, how very much that young man had improved since his first arrival at Cressingham.

With Rhoda, in the absence of her grandmother, he was an entirely different being. A great deal of apparent interest in herself, and deference to her opinions; a very little skilful flattery, too delicately administered for its hollowness to be perceived; a quick apprehension of what pleased and amused her, and a ready adaptation to her mood of the moment—these were Mr Welles' tactics with the heiress for whom he was angling. As to Phoebe, he simply let her alone. He soon saw that she was of no account in Rhoda's eyes, and was not her chosen *confidante*, but simply the person to whom she talked for want of any other listener. There was not, therefore, in his opinion, any reason why he should trouble himself to propitiate Phoebe.

Ever since the visit of the Delawarrs, Rhoda had seemed disinclined for another call on Mrs Dorothy Jennings. Now

Emily Sarah Holt

and then she went to see Mrs Clarissa, when the conversation usually turned on the fashions and cognate topics; sometimes she drank tea with Lady Betty, whose discourse was of rather a more sensible character. Rarely, she looked in on Mrs Marcella. Mrs Jane had thoroughly estranged her by persisting in her sarcastic nickname for Rhoda's chosen hero, and letting off little shafts against him, more smart than nattering. On Mrs Darcy she called perpetually, perhaps with a view to meet him at her house; but all Mr Welles' alleged devotion to his dear Aunt Eleanor scarcely ever seemed to result in his going to see her at the Maidens' Lodge. When Rhoda met him, which she very often did, it was either by his calling at the Abbey, or by an accidental *rencontre*—if accidental it were—in some secluded glade of the Park.

At length, one day, without any warning, a horse cantered up to the side door, and Molly Delawarr's voice in its loudest tones (and very loud they were) demanded where all those stupid creatures were who ought to be there to take her horse. Then Miss Molly, having been helped off, came marching in, and greeted her friends with a recitative—

"Lucy Locket lost her pocket; 'Kitty Fisher found it!'"

"My dear Mrs Molly, I am quite rejoiced to see you!"

"No! you aren't, are you?" facetiously responded Molly. "Rhoda—I vow, child, you're uglier than ever!—mother wants you for a while. There's that jade Betty going to come of age, and she means to make the biggest fuss over it ever was heard. She said she would send Wilson over, but I jumped on my tit, and came to tell you myself. You'll come, won't you, old hag?"

Rhoda looked at her grandmother.

"My dear, of course you will go!" responded Madam, "since my Lady Delawarr is so good. 'Tis so kind in Mrs Molly to take thus much trouble on herself."

"Fiddle-de-dee!" ejaculated Molly. "I'm no more kind than she's good. She wants a fuss, and a lot of folks to make it; and I wanted a ride, and some fun with Rhoda. Where's the goodness, eh?"

"Shall I take Phoebe?" asked Rhoda, doubtfully.

"You'd better," returned Molly, before Madam could speak. "You'll want somebody to curl your love-locks and stitch your fal-lals; and I'm not going to do it—don't you fancy so. Oh, I say, Rhoda! you may have Marcus Welles, if you want him. There's another fellow turned up, with a thousand a year more, that will suit me better."

"Indeed! I thank you!" said Rhoda, with a little toss of her head.

"My dear Mrs Molly, you are so diverting," smiled Madam.

"You don't say so!" rejoined that fascinating young person. "You'll put on your Sunday bombazine, Rhoda. We're all going to be as fine as fiddlers. As for you"—and Molly's bold eyes surveyed Phoebe, seeming to take in the whole at a glance—"it won't matter. You aren't an heiress, so you can come in rags."

Phoebe said nothing.

"I don't think," went on Molly, in a reflective tone, "that you can make a catch; but you can try. There is the chaplain—horrid old centipede! And there's old Walford"—Molly never favoured any man with a Mr to his name—"an ugly, spiteful old bear that nobody'll have: he's rich enough; and he might look your way if you play your cards well. Any way, you'll not have much chance else; so you'd better keep your eyes pretty well open. Now, Rhoda, come along, and we'll have some fun."

And away went Molly and Rhoda, with a smiling assent from Madam.

What a very repulsive, vulgar disagreeable girl this Molly Delawarr is! True, my gentle reader. And yet—does she do much more than say, in plain language, what a great number of Mollys are not ashamed to think?

Phoebe's sensations, in view of the coming visit to the Court, were far removed from pleasure. Must she go? She braced up her courage, and ventured to ask.

"If you please, Madam—"

"Well, child?" was the answer, in a sufficiently gracious tone to encourage Phoebe to proceed.

"Must I go with Mrs Rhoda to Delawarr Court, if you please, Madam?"

"Why, of course, child." Madam's tone expressed surprise, though not displeasure.

Phoebe swallowed her regret with a sigh, and tried to comfort herself with the thought of meeting Gatty, which was the only bright spot in the darkness. But would Gatty be there?

Rhoda and Molly came in to tea arm-in-arm.

"And how has my Lady Delawarr her health, Mrs Molly?" inquired Madam, as she poured out the refreshing fluid.

Molly had allowed no time for inquiries on her first appearance.

"Oh, *she's* well enough," said Molly, carelessly.

"And Mrs Betty is now fully recovered of her distemper?"

"She's come out of the small-pox, and tumbled into the vapours," said Molly.

"The vapours" was a most convenient term of that day. It covered everything which had no other name, from a pain in the toe to a pain in the temper, and was very frequently descriptive of the latter ailment. Betty's condition, therefore, as subject to this malady, excited little regret.

"And how goes it with Mrs Gatty? Is she now my Lady Polesworth?"

"My Lady Fiddlestrings!" responded Molly. "Not she—never will. Old Polesworth wanted a pretty face, and after Gatty's small-pox, why, you couldn't—"

"Small-pox!" cried Madam and Rhoda in concert.

"What, didn't you know?" answered Molly. "To be sure—took it the minute she got home. But that wasn't all, neither. Old Polesworth told Mum"—which meant Lady Delawarr—"that he might have stood small-pox, but he couldn't saintship; so Saint Gatty lost her chance, and much she'll ever see of such another. Dad and Mum were as mad as hornets. Dad said he'd have horsewhipped her if she'd been out of bed. Couldn't, *in* bed, you see—wouldn't have looked well."

"But, my dear, she could not help taking the small-pox?"

"Maybe not, but she might have helped taking the saint-pox," said Molly. "I believe she caught it from you," nodding at Phoebe. "But what vexed Mum most was that the grey goose actually made believe to be pleased when she lost her chance of the tinsel. Trust me, but Mum blew her up—a little! All leather and prunella, you know, of course. Pleased to be an old maid!—just think, what nonsense. She will be an old maid now, sure as eggs are eggs, unless she marries some conventicle preacher. That would be the best end of her, I should think."

Phoebe sat wondering why Molly paid so poor a compliment to her own denomination as to suppose that the natural gravitation of piety was towards Dissent. But Molly's volatile nature passed to a different subject the next moment.

"I say, old Roadside, bring a white gown. The Queen's coming to the Bath, and a lot of folks are trying to make her come on to Berkeley; and if she do, a whole parcel of young gentlewomen are to be there to courtesy to her, and give her a posy, and all that sort of flummery. And Mum says she'll send us down, if they do it."

"Who's to give the posy?" eagerly asked Rhoda.

"Don't know. Not you. You won't have a chance, old Fid-fad. No more shan't I. It'll be some thing of quality. I'll tread on her tail, though,—see if I don't."

"Whose?" whispered Rhoda; for Molly's last remark had

been confidential. "You don't mean the Queen?"

"Of course I do,—who better? Her grandmother was a baronet's daughter; what else am I? I'll have a snip of her gown, if I can."

"O Molly!" exclaimed Rhoda in unfeigned horror.

"Why not? I've scissors in my pocket."

"Molly, you never could!"

"Don't you lay much on those odds, my red currant bush. I can do pretty near anything I've a mind—when I *have* a mind."

Rhoda was not pleased by Molly's last vocative, which she took as an uncomplimentary allusion to the faint shade of red in her hair,—a subject on which she was peculiarly sensitive. This bit of confidence had been exchanged out of the hearing of Madam, who had gone to a cabinet at the other end of the long room, but within that of Phoebe, who grew more uncomfortable every moment.

"Well, 'tis getting time to say ta-ta," said Molly, rising shortly after tea was over. "Where's that tit of mine?"

"My dear, I will send to fetch your horse round," said Madam, "Pray, make my compliments to my Lady Delawarr, and tell her that I cannot but be very sensible of her kindness in offering Rhoda so considerable a pleasure."

Madam was about to add more, but Molly broke in.

"Come now! Can't carry all that flummery. My horse would fall lame under the weight. I'll say you did the pretty thing.

Ta-ta! See you on Monday, old gentlewoman." She turned to Rhoda; threw a nod, without words, to Phoebe, and five minutes afterwards was trotting across the Park on her way home to Delawarr Court.

CHAPTER SEVEN

DELAWARR COURT

"Le coeur humain a beaucoup de plis et de replis."

Madame de Motteville.

"And how goes it, my dear, with Madam and Mrs Rhoda?" inquired little Mrs Dorothy as she handed a cup to Phoebe.

"They are well, I thank you. Mrs Dolly, I have come to ask your counsel."

"Surely, dear child. Thou shalt have the best I can give. What is thy trouble?"

"I have two or three troubles," said Phoebe, sighing. "You know Rhoda is going to-morrow to Delawarr Court; and I am to go with her. I wish I need not!"

"Why, dear child?"

"Well, I am afraid it must sound silly," answered Phoebe, with a little laugh at herself; "but really, I can scarce tell why. Do you never feel thus unwilling to do a thing, Mrs Dorothy, almost without reason?"

"Ah, there is a reason," said the old lady: "and it comes either from your body or your mind, Phoebe. If 'tis from your body, let your mind govern it in any matter you *must* do. If it come from your mind, either you see a clear cause for it, or you do not."

"I do not, Mrs Dolly. I reckon 'tis but the spleen."

Everything we call nervous then fell under the head of spleen.

"There is an older name for that, Phoebe, without it arise from some disorder of the body."

"What, Mrs Dorothy?"

"Discontent, my child."

"But that is sin!" said Phoebe, looking up, as if startled.

"Ay. 'Whatsoever is not of faith is sin.'"

"Then should I be willing to go, Mrs Dolly?"

"What hast thou asked, my dear? Should God's child be willing to do her Father's will?"

Phoebe's face became grave.

"Dear Phoebe, 'when the people murmured, it displeased the Lord.' Have a care!—Well, what is your next trouble?"

"I have had a letter from mother," said Phoebe, colouring and looking uncomfortable.

"Is that a trouble, child?"

"No,—not that. Oh no! But—"

"But a trouble sticks to it. Well,—what?"

"She says I ought to—to get married, Mrs Dorothy; and she looks for me to do it while I tarry at White-Ladies, for she reckons that will be the best chance."

Mrs Dorothy was silent. If her thoughts were not complimentary to Mrs Latrobe, she gave no hint of it to Phoebe.

"I don't think I should like it, please, Mrs Dorothy," said Phoebe uneasily. "And ought I?"

"I suppose somebody had better ask you first," was Mrs Dorothy's dry answer.

"I would rather live with Mother," continued Phoebe. And suddenly a cry broke out which had been repressed till then. "I wish—oh, I wish Mother loved me! She never seemed to do it but once, when I was ill of the fever. I do so wish Mother could love me!"

Mrs Dorothy busied herself for a moment in putting the cups together on her little tea-tray. Then she came over to Phoebe.

"Little maid!" she said, lovingly, "there are some of us women for whom no love is safe, saving the love of Him that died for us. If we have it otherwise, we go wrong and set up idols in our hearts. Art thou one of those, Phoebe?"

"I don't know!" sobbed Phoebe. "How can I know?"

"Dear child, He knows. Canst thou not trust Him? 'Dieu est ton Berger.' The Shepherd takes more care of the sheep, Phoebe, than the sheep take care of themselves. Poor,

Emily Sarah Holt

blundering creatures that we are! always apt to think, in the depth of our hearts, that God would rather not save us, and that we shall have to take a great deal of trouble to persuade Him to do it. Nay! it is the Shepherd that longs to have the lamb safe folded, and the poor silly lamb that is always straying away. Phoebe, 'the Father Himself loveth thee.'"

"Oh, I know! But I can't see Him, Mrs Dorothy."

"I suppose He knows that, too," answered her old friend, softly. "He knows how much easier it would be to believe if we could see and feel. Maybe 'tis therefore He hath pronounced so special a blessing upon such as have not seen, and yet have believed."

"Mrs Dorothy,"—and Phoebe looked up earnestly,—"don't you think living is hard work?"

"I did once, my maid. But I am beyond the burden and the heat of the day now. My tools are gathered together and put away, and I am waiting for the Master to call me in home to my rest. Thou too wilt come to that, child, if thy life be long enough. And to some, even here,—to all, afterward,—it is given to see where the turns were taken in the path, and whereto the road should have led that we took not. Ah, child, one day thy heaviest cause of thankfulness may be that in this or that matter—perchance in the matter that most closely engaged thee in this life—thy Father did not give thee the desire of thine heart."

"Yet that is promised as a blessing?" said Phoebe, interrogatively, looking up.

"As a blessing, dear child, when thy will is God's will. Can it be any blessing, when thy will and His run contrary the one to the other?"

"Then you think I should not wish to be loved!" said Phoebe, with a heavy sigh.

"I think God's child will do well to leave the choice of all things to her Father."

"I must leave it. He will have it."

"He will have it," repeated Mrs Dorothy solemnly; "but, Phoebe, you can leave it in loving submission, or you can have it wrenched from you in judgment. Though it may be that you must loose your hold on a gem, yet you please yourself whether you yield it as a gift, or wait to have it torn away."

"I see," said Phoebe.

"Was there any further trouble, my dear?"

"Only that," replied Phoebe. "Life seems hard. I get so tired!"

"Thou art young to know that, child," said Mrs Dorothy, with a rather sad smile.

"Well, I don't know," answered Phoebe, doubtfully. "I think I have always been tired. And don't you know some people rest you, and some people don't? When there is nobody that rests one—Father used—but—"

Mrs Dorothy thought there was not much difficulty in reading the story hidden behind Phoebe's broken sentences.

"So life is hard?" she echoed. "Poor child! Dear, it was harder to Him that sat on the well at Sychar, wearied with His journey. He has not forgotten it, Phoebe. Couldst thou not go and remind Him of it, and ask Him to bless and rest thee?"

"Mrs Dolly, do you feel tired like that?"

A little amused laugh was Mrs Dolly's answer.

"Thou hast not all the sorrows of life in thine own portion, little Phoebe. I have felt it. I do not often now. The journey is too near at an end to fret much over the hard fare or the rough road. When there be only a few days to pass ere you leave school, your mind is more set on the coming holidays than on the length or hardness of the lessons that lie betwixt."

"I wish I hadn't to go to Delawarr Court!" sighed Phoebe. "There will be a great parcel of people, and not one I know but Rhoda, and Mrs Gatty, and Mrs Molly; and Rhoda always snubs me when Mrs Molly's there."

"Molly is trying," admitted the old lady. "But I think, dear child, you might make a friend of Gatty."

"Perhaps," said Phoebe.

"And, Phoebe, strive against discontent," said Mrs Dorothy; adding, with a smile, "and call it discontent, and not vapours. There is a great deal in giving names to things. So long as you call your pride self-respect and high spirit, you will reckon yourself much better than you are; and so long as you call your discontent low spirits or vapours, you will reckon yourself worse used than you are. Don't split on that rock, Phoebe. The worst thing you can do with wounds is to keep pulling off the bandage to see how they are getting on; and the worst thing you can do with griefs and wrongs is to nurse them and brood over them. Carry them to the Lord and show them to Him, and ask His help to bear them or right them, as

He chooses; and then forget all about them as fast as you can. Dear old Scots Davie gave me that counsel, and through fifty years I have proved how good it was."

"You never finished your story, Mrs Dolly," suggested Phoebe.

"I did not, my dear. Yet there was little to finish. I did but tarry at Court till the great plague-time, when all was broke up, and I went home to nurse my mother, who took the plague and died of it. After that I continued to dwell with my father. For a while after my mother's death, he was very low and melancholical, saying that God had now met with him and was visiting his old sins upon him. And then, the very next year, came the fire, and we were burned out and left homeless. Then he was worse than ever. 'Twas like the curse pronounced on David, said he, that the sword should never depart from his house: he could never look to know rest nor peace any more; God hated him, and pursued him to the death. No word of mine, though I strove to find many from the Word of God, seemed to bring him any comfort at all. They were not for him, he said, but for them toward whom God had purposes of mercy, and there was none for him. He had sinned against light and knowledge; and God would none of him any more.

"One morning, about a week after the fire, as I was coming back from my marketing to the little mean lodging where we had took shelter, and was just going in at the door, I was sorely started to feel a great warm hand on my shoulder, and a loud, cheery voice saith, 'Dolly Jennings, whither away so fast thou canst not see an old friend?' I looked up, and there was dear old Farmer Ingham, in his thick boots and country homespun; but I declare to you, child, that in my trouble his face was to me as that of an angel of God. I brake down, and sobbed aloud. 'Come, come, now!' saith he, comfortably; 'not

Emily Sarah Holt

so bad as that, is it? I've been seeking thee these four days, Dolly, child. I knew I could find thee if I came myself, though the Missis said I never should; and I've asked at one, and asked at another, and looked up streets and down streets, till this morning I saw a young maid, with her back to me, a-going down an alley; and says I, right out loud, "That's Dolly's back, or else I'm a Dutchman!" So I ran after thee, and only just catched thee up. I'm not so lissome as thou; nay, nor so lissome as I was at thy years. However, here I am, and here thou art; so that's all right. And there's a good bed and a warm welcome for everyone of you at Ingle Nook'—that was the name of his farm, my dear—'and I've brought up a cart and the old tit to drag it, and we'll see if we can't make thee laugh and be rosy again.' Dear old man! no nay would he take, nor suffer so much as a word from father about our being any cost and trouble to him. 'Stuff and nonsense!' said he; 'I've got money saved, and the farm's doing well, and only my two bits of maids to leave it to; and who should I desire to help in this big trouble, if not my own foster-child, and hers?' So father yielded, and we went down to Ingle Nook.

"Farmer Ingham very soon found what was wrong with father. 'Eh, poor soul!' said he to me, 'he's the hundredth sheep that's got lost out on the moor, and he reckons the Shepherd'll bide warm in the fold with the ninety and nine, and never give a thought to him, poor, starved, straying thing! Dear, dear!—and as if *I'd* do such a thing, sinner that I am!—as if I could eat a crust in peace till I'd been after my sheep, poor wretch!—and to think the good Lord'd do it!— and the poor thing a-bleating out there, and wanting to get home! Dear, dear! how we poor sinners do wrong the good Lord!' I said, 'Won't you say a word to him, daddy?' That was what I had always called him, my dear, since I was a little child. 'Eh, child!' says he, 'what canst thou be thinking on? The like of me to preach to a parson, all regular done up, bands and cassock and shovel hat and all! But I'll tell thee what—there's Dr Bates a-coming to bide with me a night this next week, on his way from the North into Sussex, and I'll ask him to edge in a word. He's a grand man, Dolly! "Silver-tongued Bates." Thou'lt hear.'

"Well, I knew, for I had heard talk of it at the time, that Dr Bates was one of them that gave up their livings when the Act of Uniformity came in, so that he was regarded as no better than a conventicler; and I wondered how father should like to be spoke to by Dr Bates any more than by Farmer Ingham, because to him they would both be laymen alike. But at that time I was learning to tarry the Lord's leisure— ah! that's a grand word, Phoebe! For His leisure runs side by side with our profit, and He'll be at leisure to attend to you the minute that you really need attending to. So I waited quietly to see what would come. Dr Bates came, and he proved to be no common hedge-preacher, but a learned man that had been to the University, and had Greek and Hebrew pat at his tongue's end. I could see that it was pleasant to father to talk with such a man; and maybe he took to him the rather because he had the look of one that had known sorrow. When a man is suffering, he will converse more readily with a fellow-sufferer than with a hale man. So they talked away of their young days, when they were at school and college, and father was much pleased, as I could see, to find that Dr Bates and he were of the same college, though not there at the same time: and a deal they had to say about this and that man, that both knew, but of course all strangers to me. I thought I had never seen Father seem to talk with the like interest and pleasure since my mother's death.

"But time went on, and their talk, and not a word from Dr Bates of the fashion I desired. I went to bed somewhat heavy. The next morning, however, as I was sat at my sewing by the parlour window—which was open, the

Emily Sarah Holt

weather being very sultry—came Dr Bates and father, and stood just beyond the window. The horse was then saddling for Dr Bates to be gone. All at once, they standing silent a moment, he laid his hand on father's shoulder, and saith very softly, "'I will hearken what the Lord God will say concerning me.'" Father turns and stares at him, as started. But he goes on, and saith, "'For the iniquity of his covetousness was I wroth, and smote him: I hid Me and was wroth, and he went on frowardly in the way of his heart. I have seen his ways, and will heal him; I will lead him also, and restore comforts unto him and to his mourners. I create the fruit of the lips. Peace, peace to him that is far off'"—he said it twice—"'peace to him that is far off, and to him that is near, saith the Lord, and I will heal him.'" He did not add one word, but went and mounted his horse, and when he had bid farewell to all else, just as he was turning away from the door, he calls out, in a cheerful voice, 'Good morning, Brother Jennings.' Then, as it were, Father seemed to awake, and he runs after, and puts his hand in Dr Bates's, who drew bridle, and for a minute they were busy in earnest discourse. Then they clasped hands again, and father saith, 'God bless you!' and away rode Dr Bates. But after that Father was different. He said to me—it was some weeks later—'Dolly, if it please God, I shall never speak another word against the men that turned out in Sixty-Two. They may have made blunders, but some at least of them were holy men of God, for all that.'"

"I was always sorry for them," said Phoebe. "And Father said so too."

"True, my dear. Yet 'tis not well we should forget that the parsons were turned out the first, and the conventiclers afterward. There were faults on both sides."

"But, Mrs Dolly, why can't good men agree?"

"Ah, child! 'They shall see eye to eye, when the Lord shall bring again Zion.' No sooner. Thank God that He looketh on the heart. I believe there may be two men in arms against each other, bitter opposers of each other, and yet each of them acting with a single eye to the honour of their Lord. He knows it, and He only, now. But how sorry they will be for their hard thoughts and speeches when they come to understand each other in the clear light of Heaven!"

"It always seems to me," said Phoebe, diffidently, "that there are a great many things we shall be sorry for then. But can anybody be sorry in Heaven?"

Mrs Dorothy smiled. "We know very little about Heaven, my dear. Less than Madam's parrot or Mrs Clarissa's dog understands about anyone writing a letter."

"Dogs do understand a great deal," remarked Phoebe. "Our Flossie did."

"My dear, I have learned no end of lessons from dogs. I only wish we Christians minded the word of our Master half as well as they do theirs. I wish men would take pattern from them, instead of starving and kicking them, or tormenting them with a view to win knowledge. We may be the higher creatures, but we are far from being the better. You may take note, too, that your dog will often resist an unpleasant thing—a dose of medicine, say—just because he does not understand why you want to give it to him, and does not know the worse thing that would otherwise befall him. Didst thou never serve thy Master like that, dear?"

"I am afraid so," said Phoebe, softly.

"We don't trust Him enough, Phoebe. It does seem as if the hardest thing in all the world was for man to trust God. You

Emily Sarah Holt

would not think I paid you much of a compliment if you heard me say, 'I'll trust Phoebe Latrobe as far as I can see her.' Yet that is what we are always doing to God. The minute we lose sight of His footsteps, we begin to murmur and question where He is taking us. But, my dear, I must not let you tarry longer; 'tis nigh sundown."

"Oh, dear!" and Phoebe looked up and rose hurriedly. "I trust Madam will not be angry. 'Tis much later than I thought."

She found Madam too busy to notice what time she returned. Rhoda's wardrobe was being packed for her visit, under the supervision of her grandmother, by the careful hands of Betty. The musk-coloured damask, which she had coveted, was the first article provided, and a cherry-coloured velvet mantle, lined with squirrel-skins, was to be worn with it. A blue satin hood completed this rather showy costume. A wadded calico wrapper, for morning wear; a hoop petticoat wider than Rhoda had ever worn before; the white dress stipulated by Molly; small lace head-dresses, instead of the old-fashioned commode; aprons of various colours, silk and satin; muslin and lace ruffles; a blue camlet riding-habit, laced with silver (ladies rode at this time dressed exactly like gentlemen, with the addition of a long skirt); and an evening dress of cinnamon-colour, brocaded with large green leaves and silver stems, with a white and gold petticoat under it— were the chief items of Rhoda's wardrobe. A new set of body-linen was also added, made of striped muslin. Since our fair ancestresses made their night-dresses of "muslin," it would appear that they extended the term to some stouter material than the thin and flimsy manufacture to which we restrict it. Rhoda's boots were of white kid, goloshed with black velvet. There were also "jessamy" gloves—namely, kid gloves perfumed with jessamine; a black velvet mask; a superb painted fan; a box of patches, another of violet powder, another of rouge, and a fourth of pomatum; one of the India scarves before alluded to; a stomacher set with garnet, a pearl necklace, and a silver box full of cachou and can-away comfits, to be taken to church for amusement during long sermons. The enamelled picture on the lid Rhoda would have done well to lay to heart, as it represented Cupid fishing for human beings, with a golden guinea on his hook. Rhoda was determined to be the finest dressed girl at Delawarr Court, and Madam had allowed her to order very much what she pleased. Phoebe's quiet mourning, new though it was, looked very mean in comparison—in her cousin's eyes.

No definite time was fixed for Rhoda's return home. She was to stay as long as Lady Delawarr wished to keep her.

"Phoebe, my dear!" said Madam.

"Madam?" responded Phoebe, with a courtesy.

"Come into my chamber; I would have a few words with you."

Phoebe followed, her heart feeling as if it would jump into her mouth. Madam shut the door, and took her seat on the cushioned settle which stretched along the foot of her bed.

"Child," she said to Phoebe, who stood modestly before her, "I think myself obliged to tell you that I expect Rhoda to settle in life on the occasion of this visit. I apprehend that she will meet with divers young gentlemen, with any of whom she might make a good match; and she can then make selection of him that will be most agreeable to her."

Phoebe privately wondered how the gentleman whom Rhoda selected was to be induced to select Rhoda.

Emily Sarah Holt

"Then," pursued Madam, "when she returns, she will tell me her design; and if on seeing the young man, and making inquiries of such as are acquainted with him, I approve of the match myself, I shall endeavour the favour of his friends, and doubt not to obtain it. Rhoda will have an excellent fortune, and she is of an agreeable turn enough. Now, my dear, at the same time, I wish you to look round you, and see if you can light on some decent man, fit for your station, that would not be disagreeable to you. I have apprised myself that Sir Richard's chaplain hath entered into no engagements, and if he were to your taste, I would do my best to settle you in that quarter, I cannot think he would prove uneasy to me, should I do him the honour; at the same time, if you find him unpleasant to you, I do not press the affair. But 'tis high time you should look out, for you have no fortune but yourself, and what I may choose to give with you: and if you order yourself after my wish, I engage myself to undertake for you—in reason, my dear, of course. The chaplain is very well paid, for Sir Richard finds him in board and a horse, and gives him beside thirty-five pound by the year, which is more than many have. He is, I learn, a good, easy man, that would not be likely to give his wife any trouble. Not very smart, but that can well be got over; and of good family, but indigent—otherwise it may well be reckoned he would not be a chaplain. So I bid you consider him well, my dear, and let me know your thoughts when you return hither."

Phoebe's thoughts just then were chasing each other in wild confusion: the principal one being that she was a victim led to the sacrifice with a rope round her neck.

"I ask your pardon, Madam; but—"

"Well, my dear, if you have something you wish to say, I am ready to listen to it," said Madam, with an air of extreme benignity.

Phoebe felt her position the more difficult because of her grandmother's graciousness. She so evidently thought herself conferring a favour on a portionless and unattractive girl, that it became hard to say an opposing word.

"If you please, Madam, and asking your pardon, must I be married?"

"Must you be married, child!" repeated Madam in astonished tones, "Why, of course you must. The woman is created for the man. You would not die a maid?"

"I would rather, if you would allow me, Madam," faltered Phoebe.

"But, my dear, I cannot allow it. I should not be doing my duty by you if I did. The woman is made for the man," repeated Madam, sententiously.

"But—was every woman made for some man, if you please, Madam?" asked poor Phoebe, struggling against destiny in the person of her grandmother.

"Of course, child—no doubt of it," said Madam.

"Then, if you please, Madam, might I not wait till I find the man I was made for?" entreated Phoebe with unconscious humour.

"When you marry a man, my dear, he is the man you were made for," oracularly replied Madam.

Phoebe was silenced, but not at all convinced, which is a very different thing. She could remember a good many husbands and wives with whom she had met who so far as she could judge, did not appear to have been created for the benefit of one another.

"And I trust you will find him at Delawarr Court. At all events, you will look out. As to waiting, my dear, at your age, and in your station, you cannot afford to wait. One or two years is no matter for Rhoda; but 'twill not serve for you. I was married before I was your age, Phoebe."

Phoebe sighed, but did not venture to speak. She felt more than ever as if she were being led to the slaughter. There was just this uncomfortable difference, that the sacrificed sheep or goat did not feel anything when once it was over, and the parallel would not hold good there. She felt utterly helpless. Phoebe knew her mother too well to venture on any appeal to her, even had she fondly imagined that representations from Mrs Latrobe would have weight with Madam. Mrs Latrobe would have been totally unable to comprehend her. So Phoebe did what was better,—carried her trial and perplexity to her Father in Heaven, and asked Him to undertake for her. Naturally shy and timid, it was a terrible idea to Phoebe that she was to be handed over bodily in this style to some stranger. Rhoda would not have cared; a change was always welcome to her, and she thought a great deal about the superior position of a matron. But in Phoebe's eyes the position presented superior responsibility, a thing she dreaded; and superior notoriety, a thing she detested. She was a violet, born to blush unseen, yet believing that perfume shed upon the desert air is not necessarily wasted.

"Here you are, old Rattle-trap!" cried Molly, from the head of the stairs, as Rhoda and Phoebe were mounting them. "Brought that white rag? We're going. Mum says so. Turn your toes out,—here's Betty."

Rhoda's hand was clasped, and her cheek kissed, by a pleasant-spoken, rather good-looking girl, very little scarred from her recent illness.

"Phoebe Latrobe?" said Betty, turning kindly to her. "I know your name, you see. I trust you will be happy here. Your chamber is this way, Rhoda."

It was a long, narrow room, with a low whitewashed ceiling, across which ran two beams. A pot-pourri stood on the little table in the centre, and there were two beds, one single and one double.

"Who's to be here beside me?" inquired Rhoda.

"Oh, Mother would have given you and Phoebe a chamber to yourselves," replied Betty, "but we are so full of company, she felt herself obliged to put in some one, so Gatty is coming to you."

"Can't it be Molly?" rather uncivilly suggested Rhoda.

Phoebe privately hoped it could not.

"Will, I think not," answered Betty, smiling. "Lady Diana Middleham wants Molly. She's in great request."

"Who is,—me?" demanded Molly, appearing as if by magic in the doorway. "Of course. I'm not going to sleep with you, Pug-nose. Not going to sleep at all. Spend the night in tickling the people I like, and running pins into those I don't. Fair warning!"

"I wonder whether it is better to be one you like, Molly, or one you don't like," said Rhoda, laughing.

"I hope you don't like me in that regard," said Betty, laughing too.

"Well, I don't particularly," was Molly's frank answer, "so you'll get the pins. Right about face! Stand—at—ease! Here comes Mum."

A very gorgeously dressed woman, all flounces and feathers as it seemed to Phoebe, sailed into the room, kissed Rhoda, told her that she was welcome, in a languishing voice, desired Betty to see her made comfortable, informed Molly that her hair was out of curl, took no notice of Phoebe, and sailed away again.

"I'm off!" Molly announced to the world. "There's Mr What-do-you-call-him downstairs. Go and have some fun with him." And Molly vanished accordingly.

Then Rhoda's unpacking had to be seen to by herself and Phoebe; that is to say, Phoebe did it, and Rhoda sat and watched her, Betty flitted about, talking to Rhoda, and helping Phoebe, till her name was called from below, and away she went to respond to it. Phoebe, at least, missed her, and thought her pleasant company. Whatever else she might be, she was good-natured. When the unpacking was finished to her satisfaction, Rhoda declared that she was perishing for hunger, and must have something before she could dress. Before she could make up her mind what to do, a rap came on the door, and a neat maid-servant entered with a tray.

"An't please you, Madam, Mrs Betty bade me bring you a dish of tea," said she; "for she said 'twas yet two good hours ere supper, and you should be the better of a snack after your journey. Here is both tea and chocolate, bread and butter, and shortcake." And setting down the tray, she left them to enjoy its contents.

"Long life to Betty!" said Rhoda. "Here, Phoebe! pour me a dish of chocolate. I never get any at home. Madam has a notion it makes people fat."

"But does she not like you to take it?" asked Phoebe, pausing, with the silver chocolatiere in her hand.

"Oh, pother! go on!" exclaimed Rhoda. "Give it me, if your tender conscience won't let you. I say, Phoebe, you'll be a regular prig and prude, if you don't mind."

"I don't know what those are," replied Phoebe, furtively engaged in rubbing her hand where Rhoda had pinched it as she seized the handle of the chocolate pot.

"Oh, don't you?" answered Rhoda. "I do, for I've got you to look at. A prig is a stuck-up silly creature, and a prude is always thinking everything wicked. And that's what you are."

Phoebe wisely made no reply. Tea finished, Rhoda condescended to be dressed and have her hair curled and powdered, gave Phoebe very few minutes for changing her own dress, and then, followed by her cousin and handmaid, she descended to the drawing-room. To Phoebe's consternation, it seemed full of young ladies and gentlemen, in fashionable array; and the consternation was not relieved by a glimpse of Mr Marcus Welles, radiant in blue and gold, through a vista of plumes, lace lappets, and fans. Betty was there, making herself generally useful and agreeable; and Molly, making herself the reverse of both. Phoebe scanned the brilliant crowd earnestly for Gatty. But Gatty was nowhere to be seen.

Rhoda went forward, and plunged into the crowd, kissing and courtesying to all the girls she recognised. She was soon the gayest of the gay among them. No one noticed Phoebe but Betty, and she gave her a kindly nod in passing, and said,

"Pray divert yourself." Phoebe's diversion was to retire into a corner, and from her "loop-hole of retreat, to peep at such a world."

A very young world it was, whose oldest inhabitant at that moment was under twenty-five. But the boys and girls—for they were little more—put on the most courtier-like and grown-up airs. The ladies sat round the room, fluttering their fans, or laughing behind them: in some cases gliding about with long trains sweeping the waxed oak floor. The gentlemen stood before them, paying compliments, cracking jokes, and uttering airy nothings. Both parties took occasional pinches of snuff. For a few minutes the scene struck Phoebe as pretty and amusing; but this impression was quickly followed by a sensation of sadness. A number of rational and immortal beings were gathered together, and all they could find to do was to look pretty and be amusing. Why, a bird, a dog, or a monkey, could have done as much, and more.

And a few words came into Phoebe's mind, practically denied by the mass of mankind then as now, "Thou hast created all things, and *for Thy pleasure* they are."

How apt man is to think that every creature and thing around him was created for *his* pleasure! or, at least, for his use and benefit. The natural result is, that he considers himself at liberty to use them just as he pleases, quite regardless of their feelings, especially when any particular advantage may be expected to accrue to himself.

But "the Lord hath made all things for Himself," and "He cometh to judge the earth."

CHAPTER EIGHT

RHODA IS TAKEN IN THE TRAP

"That busy hive, the world,
And all its thousand stings."

Phoebe sat still for a while in her corner, watching the various members of the party as they flitted in and out: for the scene was now becoming diversified by the addition of elder persons. Ere long, two gentlemen in evening costume, engaged in conversation, came and stood close by her. One of them, as she soon discovered, was Sir Richard Delawarr.

"'Tis really true, then," demanded the other—a round-faced man, with brilliant eyes, who was attired as a dignitary of the Church—"'tis really true, Sir, that the Queen did forbid the visit of the Elector?"

"*I* had it from an excellent hand, I assure you," returned Sir Richard. "Nor only that, but the Princess Sophia so laid it to heart, that 'twas the main cause of her sudden death."

"It really was so?"

"Upon honour, my Lord; my Lady Delawarr had it from Mrs Rosamond Harley."

"Ha! then 'tis like to be true. You heard, I doubt not, Sir, of D'Urfey's jest on the Princess Sophia?—ha, ha, ha!" and the Bishop laughed, as if the recollection amused him exceedingly.

"No, I scarce think I did, my Lord."

"Not? Ah, then, give me leave to tell it you. I hear it gave the Queen extreme diversion.

> "'The crown is too weighty
> For shoulders of eighty—
> She could not sustain such a trophy:
> Her hand, too, already
> Has grown so unsteady,
> She can't hold a sceptre:
> So Providence kept her
> Away—poor old dowager Sophy!'"

Sir Richard threw his head back, and indulged in unfeigned merriment. Phoebe, in her corner, felt rather indignant. Why should the Princess Sophia, or any other woman, be laughed at solely for growing old?

"Capital good jest!" said the Baronet, his amusement over. "I heard from a friend that I met at the Bath, that the Queen is looking vastly well this summer—quite rid of her gout."

"So do I hear," returned the Bishop. "What think you of the price set on the Pretender's head?"

Sir Richard whistled.

"The Queen's own sole act, without any concurrence of her Ministers," continued the Bishop.

"Dear, dear!" exclaimed Sir Richard. "Five thousand, I was told?"

"Five thousand. An excellent notion, I take it."

"Well—I—don't—know!" slowly answered Sir Richard. "I cannot but feel very doubtful of the mischievous consequence that may ensue. A price on the head of the Prince of Wales! Sounds bad, my Lord—sounds bad! Though, indeed, he be not truly the Queen's brother, yet 'tis unnatural for his sister to set a price on his head."

By which remark it will be seen that Sir Richard's intellect was not of the first order. The intellect of Bishop Atterbury was: and a slightly contemptuous smile played on his lips for a moment.

"'The Prince of Wales!'" repeated he. "Surely, Sir, you have more wit than to credit that baseless tale? Why not set a price on the Pretender?"

Be it known to the reader, though it was not to Sir Richard, that on that very morning Bishop Atterbury had forwarded a long letter to the Palace of Saint Germain, in which he addressed the aforesaid Pretender as "your Majesty," and assured him of his entire devotion to his interests.

"Oh, come, I leave the whys and wherefores to yon gentlemen of the black robe!" answered Sir Richard, laughing. "By the way, talking of prices, have you heard the prodigious price Sir Nathaniel Fowler hath given for his seat in the Commons? Six thousand pounds, 'pon my honour!"

"Surely, Sir, you have been misinformed. Six thousand! 'Tis amazing."

Emily Sarah Holt

"Your Lordship may well say so. Why, I gave but eight hundred for mine. By the way, there is another point I intended to acquaint you of, my Lord. Did you hear, ever, that there should be a little ill-humour with my Lord Oxford, on account of—you know?"

"On account? Oh!" and the Bishop's right hand was elevated to his lips, in the attitude of a person drinking. "Yes, yes. Well, I cannot say I am entirely ignorant of that affair. Sir Jeremy's lady assured me she knew, beyond contradiction, that my Lord Oxford once waited on her, somewhat foxed."

Of course, "she" was the Queen. But why a fox, usually as sober a beast as others, should have been compelled to lend its name to the vocabulary of intoxication, is not so apparent.

"Absolutely drunk, I heard," responded Sir Richard; "and she was prodigiously angered. Said to my Lady Masham, that if it were ever repeated, she would take his stick from him that moment. Odd, if the ministry were to fall for such a nothing as that."

"Well, 'twas not altogether reverential to the sovereign," said the Bishop; "and the Queen is extreme nice, you know."

The threat of taking the stick from a minister was less figurative in Queen Anne's days than now. The white wand of office was carried before every Cabinet Minister, not only in his public life, but even in private.

At this point a third gentleman joined the others, and they moved away, leaving Phoebe in her corner.

Phoebe sat meditating, for nobody had spoken to her, when she felt a soft gloved hand laid upon her arm. She turned, suddenly, to look up into a face which she thought at first was the face of a stranger. Then, in a moment, she knew Gatty Delawarr.

The small-pox had changed her terribly—far more than her sister. No one could think of setting her up for a beauty now. The soft, peach-like complexion, which had been Gatty's best point, was replaced by a sickly white, pitifully seamed with the scars of the dread disease.

"You did not know me at first," said Gatty, quietly, as if stating a fact, not making an inquiry.

"I do now," answered Phoebe, returning Gatty's smile.

"Well, you see the Lord made a way for me. But it is rather a rough one, Phoebe."

"I am afraid you must have suffered *very* much, Mrs Gatty."

"Won't you drop the Mistress? I would rather. Well, yes, I suffered, Phoebe; but it was worse since than just then."

Phoebe's face, not her tongue, said, "In what manner?"

"'Tis not very pleasant, Phoebe, to have everybody bewailing you, and telling all their neighbours how cruelly you are changed, but I could have stood that. Nor is it delightful to have Molly for ever at one's elbow, calling one Mrs Baboon, and my Lady Venus, and such like; but I could have stood that, though I don't like it. But 'tis hard to be told I have disappointed my mother's dearest hopes, and that she will never take any more pleasure in me; that she would to Heaven I had died in my cradle. That stings sometimes. Then, to know that if one makes the least slip, it will be directly, 'Oh, your saints are no better than other folks!' Phoebe, I wish sometimes that I had not recovered."

Emily Sarah Holt

"Oh, but you must not do that, Mrs Gatty!—well, Gatty, then, as you are so kind. The Lord wanted you for something, I suppose."

"I wonder for what!" said Gatty.

"Well, we can't tell yet, you see," replied Phoebe, simply. "I suppose you will find out by and bye."

"I wish I could find out," said Gatty, sighing.

"I think He will show you, when He is ready," said Phoebe. "Father used to say that it took a good deal longer to make a fine microscope than it did to make a common chisel or hammer; and he thought it was the same with us. I mean, you know, that if the Lord intends us to do very nice work, He will be nice in getting us ready for it, and it may take a good while. And father used to say that we seldom know what God is doing with us while He does it, but only when He has finished."

"Nice," at that time, had not the sense of pleasant, but only that of delicately particular.

"I am glad you have told me that, Phoebe. I wish your father had been living now."

"Oh!" very deep-drawn, from Phoebe, echoed the wish.

"Phoebe, I want you to tell me where you get your patience?"

"My patience!" repeated astonished Phoebe.

"Yes; I think you are the most patient maid I know."

"I can't tell you, I am sure!" answered Phoebe, in a rather

puzzled tone. "I didn't know I was patient. I don't think I have often asked for that, specially. Very often, I ask God to give me what He sees I need; and if that be as you say, I suppose He saw I wanted it, and gave it me."

The admiring look in Gatty's eyes was happily unintelligible to Phoebe.

"Now then!" said Molly's not particularly welcome voice, close by them. "Here's old Edmundson. Clasp your hands in ecstasy, Phoebe. Mum says you and he have got to fall in love and marry one another; so make haste about it. He's not an ill piece, only you'll find he won't get up before noon unless you squirt water in his face. Now then, fall to, and say some pretty things to one another!"

Of course Molly had taken the most effectual way possible to prevent any such occurrence. Phoebe did not dare to lift her eyes; and the chaplain was, if possible, the shyer of the two, and had been dragged there against his will by invincible Molly. Neither would have known what to do, if Gatty had not kindly come to the rescue.

"Pray sit down, Mr Edmundson," she said, in a quiet, natural way, as if nothing had happened. "I thought I had seen you riding forth, half an hour ago; I suppose it must have been some one else."

"I—ah—yes—no, I have not been riding to-day," stammered the perturbed divine.

"Twas a very pleasant morning for a ride," said mediating Gatty.

"Very pleasant, Madam," answered the chaplain.

"Have you quite lost your catarrh, Mr Edmundson?"

"Quite, I thank you, Madam."

"I believe my mother wishes to talk with you of Jack Flint, Mr Edmundson."

"Yes, Madam?"

"The lad hath been well spoken of to her for the under-gardener's boy's place. I think she wished to have your opinion of him."

"Yes, Madam."

"Is the boy of a choleric disposition?"

"Possibly, Madam."

"But what think you, Mr Edmundson?"

"Madam, I—ah—I cannot say, Madam."

"I think I see Mr Lamb beckoning to you," observed Gatty, wishful to relieve the poor *gauche* chaplain from his uncomfortable position.

"Madam, I thank you—ah—very much, Madam." And Mr Edmundson made a dive into the throng, and disappeared behind a quantity of silk brocade and Brussels lace. Phoebe ventured to steal a glance at him as he departed. She found that the person to whom she had been so unceremoniously handed over, alike by Madam, Lady Delawarr, and Molly, was a thickset man of fifty years, partially bald, with small, expressionless features. He was not more fascinating to look at than to talk to, and Phoebe could only entertain a faint hope that his preaching might be an improvement upon both looks and conversation.

A little later in the evening, as Phoebe sat alone in her corner, looking on, "I say!" came from behind her. Her heart fluttered, for the voice was Molly's.

"I say!" repeated Molly. "You look here. I'm not all bad, you know. I didn't want old Edmundson to have you. And I knew the way to keep him from it was to tell him he must. I think 'tis a burning shame to treat a maid like that. They were all set on it—the old woman, and Mum, and everybody. He's an old block of firewood. You're fit for something better. I tease folks, but I'm not quite a black witch. Ta-ta. *He'll* not tease you now."

And Molly disappeared as suddenly as she had appeared. There was no opportunity for Phoebe to edge in a word. But, for once in her life, she felt obliged to Molly.

The next invader of Phoebe's peace was Lady Delawarr herself. She sat down on an ottoman, fanned herself languidly, and hoped dear Mrs Rhoda was enjoying herself.

Phoebe innocently replied that she hoped so too.

"'Twill be a pretty sight, all the young maids in white, to meet the Queen at Berkeley," resumed Lady Delawarr. "There are fourteen going from this house. My three daughters, of course, and Lady Diana—she is to hand the nosegay—and Mrs Rhoda, and Mrs Kitty Mainwaring, and Mrs Sophia Rich, and several more. Those that do not go must have some little pleasure to engage them whilst the others are away. I thought they might drink a dish of chocolate in yon little ivy-covered tower in the park, and have the young gentlemen to wait on them and divert them.

The four gentlemen of the best families and fortunes will wait on the gentlewomen to Berkeley: that is, Mr Otway, Mr Seymour, my nephew Mr George Merton, and Mr Welles. I shall charge Mr Derwent yonder to wait specially on you, Mrs Phoebe, while Mrs Rhoda is away."

Phoebe perceived that she was not one of the fourteen favoured ones. A little flutter of anxiety disturbed her anticipations. What would go on with Rhoda and Mr Welles?

Lady Delawarr sat for a few minutes, talking of nothing in particular, and then rose and sailed away. It was evident that the main object of her coming had been to give Phoebe a hint that she must not expect to join the expedition to Berkeley.

As Phoebe went upstairs that evening, feeling rather heavy-hearted, she saw something gleam and fall, and discovered, on investigation, that a tassel had dropped from Rhoda's purse, which that young lady had desired her to carry up for her. She set to work to hunt for it, but for some seconds in vain. She had almost given up the search in despair, when a strange voice said behind her, "Le voici, Mademoiselle."

Phoebe turned and faced her countrywoman—for so she considered her—with an exclamation of delight.

"Ah! you speak French, Mademoiselle?" said the girl. "It is a pleasure, a pleasure, to hear it!"

"I am French," responded Phoebe, warmly. "My father was a Frenchman. My name is Phoebe Latrobe: what is yours?"

"Louise Dupret. I am Lady Delawarr's woman. I have been here two long, long years; and nobody speaks French but Madame and Mesdemoiselles her daughters. And Mademoiselle Marie will not, though she can. She will talk to me in English, and laughs at me when I understand her not. Ah, it is dreadful!"

"From what part of France do you come?"

"From the mountains of the Cevennes. And you?"

"The same. Then you are of the religion?"

This was the Huguenot form of inquiry whether a stranger belonged to them. Louise's eyes lighted up.

"We are daughters of the Church of the Desert," she said. "And we are sisters in Jesus Christ."

From that hour Phoebe was not quite friendless at Delawarr Court. It was well for her: since the preparations for Berkeley absorbed Gatty, and of Rhoda she saw nothing except during the processes of dressing and undressing. Very elaborate processes they became, for Lady Delawarr kept a private hair-dresser, who came round every morning to curl, friz, puff, and powder each young lady in turn; and the unfortunate maiden who kept him waiting an instant was relegated to the last, and certain to be late for breakfast. Following in the footsteps of his superiors, he did not notice Phoebe, nor count her as one of the group; but after the meeting on the stairs, as soon as Lady Delawarr released her, Louise was at hand with a beaming face, entreating permission to arrange Mademoiselle, and she sent her down-stairs looking very fresh and stylish, almost enough to provoke the envy of Rhoda.

"Ah, Mademoiselle!—if you were but a rich, rich lady, and I might be your maid!" sighed Louise. "This is a dreary world; and a dreary country, this England; and a dreary house, this Cour de la Warre! Madame is—is—ah, well, she is my

Emily Sarah Holt

mistress, and it is not right to chatter all one thinks. Still one cannot help thinking. Mademoiselle Betti—if she were in my country, we should call her Elise, which is pretty—it is ugly, Betti!—well, Mademoiselle Betti is very good-natured—very, indeed; and Mademoiselle Henriette—ah, this droll country! her name is Henriette, and they call her Gatti!—she is very good, very good and pleasant Mademoiselle Henriette. And since she had the small-pox she is nicer than before. It had spoiled her face to beautify her heart. Ah, that poor demoiselle, how she suffers! Perhaps, Mademoiselle, it is not right that I should tell you, even you; but she suffers so much, this good demoiselle, and she is so patient! But for Mademoiselle Marie—ah, there again the droll name, Molli!—does not Mademoiselle think this a strange, very strange, country?"

The great expedition was ready to set out at last. All the girls were dressed exactly alike, in white, and all the gentlemen in blue turned up with white. They were to travel in two coaches to Bristol, where all were to sleep at the house of Mrs Merton, sister-in-law to Lady Delawarr; the next day the bouquet was to be presented at Berkeley, and on the third day they were to return. By way of chaperone, the house-keeper at the Court was to travel with them to and from Bristol, out Mrs Merton herself undertook to conduct them to Berkeley.

Rhoda was in the highest spirits, and Phoebe saw her assisted into the coach by Mr Marcus Welles with no little misgiving. Molly, as she brushed past Phoebe, allowed the point of a steel scissors-sheath to peep from her pocket for an instant, accompanying it with the mysterious intimation—"You'll see!"

"What will she see, Molly?" asked Lady Diana, who was close beside her.

"How to use a pair of scissors," said Molly. "What's to be cut, Molly?" Sophia Rich wished to know.

"A dash!" said Molly, significantly. And away rolled the coaches towards Bristol. Phoebe turned back into the house with a rather desolate feeling. For three days everybody would be gone. Those who were left behind were all strangers to her except Mr Edmundson, and she wanted to get as far from him as she could. True, there was Louise; but Louise could hardly be a companion for her, even had her work for Lady Delawarr allowed it, for she was not her equal in education. The other girls were engaged, as usual, in idle chatter, and fluttering of fans. Lady Delawarr, passing through the room, saw Phoebe sitting rather disconsolately in a corner.

"Mrs Phoebe, my dear, come and help me to make things ready for to-morrow," she said, good-naturedly; and Phoebe followed her very willingly.

The picnic was a success. The weather was beautiful, and the young people in good temper—two important points. Lady Delawarr herself, in the absence of her housekeeper, superintended the packing of the light van which carried the provisions to the old tower. There was to be a gipsy fire to boil the kettle, with three poles tied together over it, from which the kettle was slung in the orthodox manner. Phoebe, who was trying to make herself useful, stretched out her hand for the kettle, when Lady Delawarr's voice said behind her, "My dear Mrs Phoebe, you may be relieved of that task. Mr Osmund Derwent—Mrs Phoebe Latrobe. Mrs Latrobe—Mr Derwent."

There was one advantage, now lost, in this double introduction; if the name were not distinctly heard in the first instance, it might be caught in the second.

Emily Sarah Holt

Phoebe looked up, and saw a rather good-looking young man, whose good looks, however, lay more in a pleasant expression than in any special beauty of feature. A little shy, yet without being awkward; and a little grave and silent, but not at all morose, he was one with whom Phoebe felt readily at home. His shyness, which arose from diffidence, not pride, wore off when the first strangeness was over. It was evident that Lady Delawarr had given him, as she had said, a hint to wait on Phoebe.

The peculiarity of Lady Delawarr's conduct rather puzzled Phoebe. At times she was particularly gracious, whilst at others she utterly neglected her. Simple, unworldly Phoebe did not guess that while Rhoda Peveril and Phoebe Latrobe were of no consequence in the eyes of her hostess, the future possessor of White-Ladies was of very much. Lady Delawarr never felt quite certain who that was to be. She expected it to be Rhoda; yet at times the conviction smote her that, after all, there was no certainty that it might not be Phoebe. Madam was impulsive; she had already surprised people by taking up with Phoebe at all; and Rhoda might displease her. In consequence of these reflections, though Phoebe was generally left unnoticed, yet occasionally Lady Delawarr warmed into affability, and cultivated the girl who might, after all, come to be the heiress of Madam's untold wealth. For Lady Delawarr's mind was essentially of the earth, earthy; gold had for her a value far beyond goodness, and pleasantness of disposition or purity of mind were not for a moment to be set in comparison with a suite of pearls.

Mr Derwent took upon himself the responsibility of the kettle, and chatted pleasantly enough with Phoebe, to whom the other damsels were only too glad to leave all trouble. He walked home with her, insisting with playful persistence upon carrying her scarf and the little basket which she had brought for wild flowers; talked to her about his mother and sisters, his own future prospects as a younger son who must make his way in the world for himself, and took pains to make himself generally agreeable and interesting. Under his kindly notice Phoebe opened like a flower to the sun. It was something new to her to find a sensible, grown-up person who really seemed to take pleasure in talking with her—except Mrs Dorothy Jennings, and she and Phoebe were not on a level. In conversation with Mrs Dorothy she felt herself being taught and counselled; in conversation with Mr Derwent she was entertained and gratified.

Judging from his conduct, Mr Derwent was as much pleased with Phoebe as she was with him. During the whole time she remained at Delawarr Court, he constituted himself her cavalier. He was always at hand when she wanted anything, at times supplying the need even before she had discovered its existence. Phoebe tasted, for the first time in her life, the flattering ease of being waited on, instead of waiting on others; the delicate pleasure of being listened to, instead of snubbed and disregarded; the intellectual treat of finding one who was willing to exchange ideas with her, rather than only to impart ideas to her. Was it any wonder if Osmund Derwent began to form a nucleus in her thoughts, round which gathered a floating island of fair fancies and golden visions, all the more beautiful because they were vague?

And all the while, Phoebe never realised what was happening to her. She let herself drift onwards in a pleasant dream, and never thought of pausing to analyse her sensations.

The absentees returned home in the afternoon of the third day. And beyond the roll of the coaches, and the noise and bustle inseparable from the arrival of eighteen persons, the first intimation of it which was given in the drawing-room was caused by the entrance of Molly, who swept into the room with tragi-comic dignity, and mounting a chair, cleared her voice, and held forth, as if it had been a sceptre, a minute bow of black gauze ribbon.

"Ladies and gentlewomen!" said Molly with solemnity. "(The gentlemen don't count.) Ladies and gentlewomen! I engaged myself, before leaving the Court, to bring back to you in triumph a snip from the Queen's gown. Behold it! (Never mind how I got it,—here it is.) Upon honour, as sure as my name is Mary—('tisn't,—I was christened Maria)— but, as sure as there is one rent and two spots of mud on this white gown which decorates my charming person,—the places whereof are best known to myself,—this bow of gauze, on which all your eyes are fixed,—now there's a shame! Sophy Rich isn't looking a bit—this bow was on the gown of Her Majesty Queen Anne yesterday morning! *Plaudite vobis*!"

And down came Miss Molly.

"If I might be excused, Mrs Maria," hesitatingly began Mr Edmundson, who seemed almost afraid of the sound of his own voice, "*vobis* is, as I cannot but be sensible, not precisely the—ah—not quite the word—ah—"

"You shut up, old Bandbox," said Molly, dropping her heroics. "None of your business. Can't you but be sensible? First time you ever were!"

"I ask your pardon, Mrs Maria. I trust, indeed,—ah—I am not—ah—insensible, to the many—ah—many things which—"

The youthful company were convulsed with laughter. They were all aware that Molly was intentionally talking at cross purposes with her pastor; and that while he clung to the old signification of sensible, namely, to be aware of, or sensitive to, a thing, she was using it in the new, now universally accepted, sense of sagacious. The fun, of course, was enhanced by the fact that poor Mr Edmundson was totally unacquainted with the change of meaning.

"I don't believe she cut it off a bit!" whispered Kitty Mainwaring. "She gave a guinea to some orange-girl who was cousin to some other maid in the Queen's laundry,—some stuff of that sort. Cut it off!—how could she? Just tell me that."

Before the last word was well out of Kitty's lips, Molly's small, bright scissors were snapped within an inch of Kitty's nose.

"Perhaps you would have the goodness to say that again, Mrs Catherine Mainwaring!" observed that young person, in decidedly menacing tones.

"Thank you, no, I don't care to do," replied Kitty, laughing, but shrinking back from the scissors.

"When I say I will do a thing, I will do it, Madam!" retorted Molly.

"If you can, I suppose," said Kitty, defending herself from another threatening snap.

"Say I can't, at your peril!"

And Molly and her scissors marched away in dudgeon.

"You are very tired, I fear, Mrs Gatty," said Phoebe, when Gatty came up to the room they shared, for the night.

Emily Sarah Holt

"Rather," answered Gatty, with a sad smile on her white face.

But she did not tell Phoebe what had tired her. It was not the journey, nor the ceremony, but her mother's greeting.

"Why, Betty, you are quite blooming!" Lady Delawarr had said. "It hath done you good, child. And Molly, too, as sprightly as ever! Child, did you get touched?"

"I did, Madam," answered Molly, with an extravagant courtesy.

"Ah!" said her mother, in a tone of great satisfaction. "Then we need apprehend no further trouble from the evil. I am extreme glad. O Gatty! you poor, scarred, wretched creature! Really, had it not been that the absence of one of my daughters would be remarked on, I vow I wish you had not gone! 'Tis such a sight to show, that dreadful face of yours. You will never give me any more comfort—that is certain."

"Pos.!" echoed Molly, exactly in the same tone.

"I would not mind, Gatty!" was Betty's kindly remark.

"Thank you," said Gatty, meekly. "I wish I did not!"

Gatty did not repeat this to Phoebe. But Phoebe saw there was something wrong.

Rhoda came rustling in before much more could be said. She was full of details of the journey. What the Queen looked like,—a tall, stout woman, with such blooming cheeks that Rhoda felt absolutely certain she wore rouge,—how she was dressed,—all in black, with a black calash, or high, loose hood, and adorned with diamonds—how she had been received,—with ringing cheers from the Tory part of the population, but ominous silence, or very faint applause, from such as were known to be Whigs: how Sophia Rich had told Rhoda that all the Whig ladies of mark had made up their minds to attend no drawing-rooms the next season: how it was beginning to be dimly suspected that Lord Mar was coquetting with the exiled members of the royal family, and more than suspected that the Duke and Duchess of Marlborough were no longer all powerful with Queen Anne, as they had once been: how the Queen always dined at three p.m., never drank French wine, held drawing-rooms on Sundays after service, would not allow any gentleman to enter her presence without a full-bottomed periwig: all these bits of information Rhoda dilated on, passing from one to another with little regard to method, and wound up with an account of the presentation of the bouquet, and how the Queen had received it from Lady Diana with a smile, and, "I thank you all, young gentlewomen," in that silver voice which was Anne's pre-eminent charm.

But half an hour later, when Gatty was asleep, Rhoda said to Phoebe,—

"I have made up my mind, Phoebe."

"Have you?" responded Phoebe. "What about?"

"I mean to marry Marcus Welles."

"Has he asked you?" said Phoebe, rather drily.

"Yes," was Rhoda's short answer.

Phoebe lay silent.

"Well?" said Rhoda, rather sharply.

"I think, Cousin, I had better be quiet," answered Phoebe; "for I am afraid I can't say what you want me."

"What I want you!" echoed Rhoda, more sharply than ever. "What do I want you to say, Mrs Prude, if you please?"

"Well, I suppose you would like me to say I was glad: and I am not: so I can't."

"I don't suppose it signifies to us whether you are glad or sorry," snapped Rhoda. "But why aren't you glad?—you never thought he'd marry you, surely?"

Phoebe said "No" with a little laugh, as she thought how very far she was from any such expectation, and how very much farther from any wish for it. But Rhoda was not satisfied.

"Well, then, what's the matter?" said she.

"Do you want me to say, Cousin?"

"Of course I do! Should I have asked you if I didn't?"

"I am afraid he does not love you."

Rhoda sat up on her elbow, with an ejaculation of amazement.

"If I ever heard such nonsense? What do you know about it, you poor little white-faced thing?"

"I dare say I don't know much about it," said Phoebe, calmly; "but I know that if a man really loves one woman with all his heart, he won't laugh and whisper and play with the fan of another, or else he is not worth anybody's love. And I am afraid what Mr Welles wants is just your money and not you.

I beg your pardon, Cousin Rhoda."

It was time. Rhoda was in a towering passion. What could Phoebe mean, she demanded with terrible emphasis, by telling such lies as those? Did she suppose that Rhoda was going to believe them? Did Phoebe know what the Bible said about speaking ill of your neighbour? Wasn't she completely ashamed of herself?

"And I'll tell you what, Phoebe Latrobe," concluded Rhoda, "I don't believe it, and I won't! I'm not going to believe it,— not if you go down on your knees and swear it! 'Tis all silly, wicked, abominable nonsense!—and you know it!"

"Well, if you won't believe it, there's an end," said Phoebe, quietly. "And I think, if you please, Cousin, we had better go to sleep."

"Pugh! Sleep if you can, you false-hearted crocodile!" said Rhoda, poetically, in distant imitation of the flowers of rhetoric of her friend Molly. "I shan't sleep to-night. Not likely!"

Yet Rhoda was asleep the first.

Emily Sarah Holt

CHAPTER NINE

SOMETHING ALTERS EVERYTHING

"To-night we sit together here,
To-morrow night shall come—ah, where?"

Robert Lord Lytton.

"There! Didn't I tell you, now?" ejaculated Mrs Jane Talbot.

"I am sure I don't know, Jane," responded her sister, in querulous tones. "You are always talking about something. I never can tell how you manage to keep continually talking, in the way you do. I could not bear it. I never was a talker; I haven't breath for it, with my poor chest,—such a perpetual rattle,—I don't know how you stand it, I'm sure. And to think what a beautiful singer I was once! Young Sir Samuel Dennis once said I entranced him, when he had heard my singing to Mrs Lucy's spinet—positively entranced him! And Lord James Morehurst—"

"An unmitigated donkey!" slid in Mrs Jane.

"Jane, how you do talk! One can't get in a word for you. What was I saying, Clarissa?"

"You were speaking of Lord James Morehurst, dear Marcella. 'Tis all very well for Jane to run him down," said Mrs Vane in a languishing style, fanning herself as she spoke, "but I am sure he was the most charming black man I ever saw. He once paid me such a compliment on my fine eyes!"

"More jackanapes he!" came from Mrs Jane.

"Well, I don't believe he ever paid you such an one," said Mrs Clarissa, pettishly.

"He'd have got his ears boxed if he had," returned Mrs Jane. "The impudence of some of those fellows!"

"Poor dear Jane! she never had any taste," sighed Mrs Marcella. "I protest, Clarissa, I am quite pleased to hear this news. As much pleased, you know, as a poor suffering creature like me can be. But I think Mrs Rhoda has done extreme well. Mr Welles is of a good stock and an easy fortune, and he has the sweetest taste in dress."

"Birds of a feather!" muttered Mrs Jane. "Ay, I knew what Mark-Me-Well was after. Told you so from the first. I marked him, be sure."

"I suppose he has three thousand a year?" inquired Mrs Clarissa.

"Guineas—very like. Not brains—trust me!" said Mrs Jane.

"And an estate?" pursued Mrs Clarissa, with languid interest.

"Oh dear, yes!" chimed in the invalid; "I would have told you about it, if Jane could ever hold her tongue. Such a—"

"I've done," observed Mrs Jane, marching off.

"Oh, my dear Clarissa, you can have no conception of what I suffer!" resumed Mrs Marcella, sinking down to a confidential tone. "I love quiet above all things, and Jane's tongue is never still. Ah! if I could go to the wedding, as I used to do! I was at all the grand weddings in the county when I was a young maid. I couldn't tell you how many times I was bridesmaid. When Sir Samuel was married—and really, after all the fine things he had said, and the way he used to ogle me through his glass, I *did* think!—but, however, that's neither here nor there. The creature he married had plenty of money, but absolutely no complexion, and she painted—oh, how she did paint! and a turn-up nose,—the ugliest thing you ever saw. And with all that, the airs she used to give herself! It really was disgusting."

"O, my dear! I can't bear people that give themselves airs," observed Mrs Clarissa, with a toss of her head, and "grounding" her fan.

"No, nor I," echoed Mrs Marcella, quite as unconscious as her friend of the covert satire in her words. "I wonder what Mrs Rhoda will be married in. I always used to say I would be married in white and silver. And really, if my wretched health had not stood in the way, I might have been, my dear, ever so many times. I am sure it would have come to something, that evening when Lord James and I were sitting in the balcony, after I had been singing,—and there, that stupid Jane must needs come in the way! I always liked a pretty wedding. I should think it would be white and silver. And what do you suppose Madam will give her?"

"Oh, a set of pearls, I should say, if not diamonds," answered Mrs Clarissa.

"She will do something handsome, of course."

"Suppose you do something handsome, and swallow your medicine without a lozenge," suggested Mrs Jane, walking in and presenting a glass to her sister. "'Tis time."

"I am sure it can't be, Jane! You are always making me swallow some nasty stuff. And as to taking it without a lozenge, I couldn't do such a thing!"

"Stuff! You could, if you did," said Mrs Jane. "Come, then,—here it is. I shouldn't want one."

"Oh, you!—you have not my fine feelings!" responded Mrs Marcella, sitting with the glass in her hand, and looking askance at its reddish-brown contents.

"Come, sup it up, and get it over," said her sister. "O Jane!—you unfeeling creature!"

"'Twill be no better five minutes hence, I'm sure."

"You see what I suffer, Clarissa!" wailed Mrs Marcella, gulping down the medicine, and pulling a terrible face. "Jane has no feeling for me. She never had. I am a poor despised creature whom nobody cares for. Well, I suppose I must bear it. 'Tis my fate. But what I ever did to be afflicted in this way! Oh, the world's a hard place, and life's a very, very dreary thing. Oh dear, dear!"

Phoebe Latrobe, who had been sent by Madam to tell the news at the Maidens' Lodge, sat quietly listening in a corner. But when Mrs Marcella began thus to play her favourite tune, Phoebe rose and took her leave. She called on Lady Betty, who expressed her gratification in the style of measured propriety which characterised her. Lastly, with a

Emily Sarah Holt

slow and rather tired step, she entered the gate of Number One. She had left her friend Mrs Dorothy to the last.

"Just in time for a dish of tea, child!" said little Mrs Dorothy, with a beaming smile. "Sit you down, my dear, and take off your hood, and I will have the kettle boiling in another minute. Well, and how have you enjoyed your visit? You look tired, child."

"Yes, I feel tired," answered Phoebe. "I scarce know how I enjoyed the visit, Mrs Dorothy—there were things I liked, and there were things I didn't like."

"That is generally the case, my dear."

"Yes," said Phoebe, abstractedly. "Mrs Dorothy, did you know Mrs Marcella Talbot when she was young?"

"A little, my dear. Not so well as I know her now."

"Was she always as discontented as she is now?"

"That is a spirit that grows on us, Phoebe," said Mrs Dorothy, gravely.

Phoebe blushed. "I know you think I have it," she replied. "But I should not wish to be like Mrs Marcella."

"I think thy temptation lies that way, dear child. But thy disposition is not so light and frivolous as hers. However, we will not talk of our neighbours without we praise them."

"Mrs Dorothy, Rhoda has engaged herself to Mr Marcus Welles. Madam sent me down to tell all of you."

"She has, has she?" responded Mrs Dorothy, as if it were

quite what she expected. "Well, I trust it may be for her good."

"Aren't you sorry, Mrs Dorothy?"

"Scarce, my dear. We hardly know what are the right things to grieve over. You and I might have thought it a very mournful thing when the prodigal son was sent into the field to feed swine: yet—speaking after the manner of men—if that had not happened, he would not have arisen and have gone to his father."

"Do you think Rhoda will have to go through trouble before she can find peace, Mrs Dorothy?"

"'Before she can—' I don't know, my dear. Before she will— I am afraid, yes."

"I am so sorry," said Phoebe.

"Dear child, the last thing the prodigal will do is to arise and go to the Father. He will try every sort of swine's husks first. He doth not value the delicates of the Father's house—he hath no taste for them. The husks are better, to his palate. What wonder, then, if he tarry yet in the far country?"

"But how are you to get him to change his taste, Mrs Dorothy?"

"Neither you nor he can do that, my dear. Most times, either the husks run short, or he gets cloyed with them. That is, if he ever go back to the Father. For some never do, Phoebe— they stay on in the far country, and find the husks sweet to the end."

"That must be saddest of all," said Phoebe, sorrowfully.

Emily Sarah Holt

"It is saddest of all. Ah, child!—thank thy Father, if He have made thy husks taste bitter."

"But all things are not husks, Mrs Dorothy!"

"Certainly not, my dear. Delight in the Lord's works in nature, or in the pleasures of the intellect such things as these are right enough in their place, Phoebe. The danger is of putting them into God's place."

"Mrs Dolly," asked Phoebe, gravely, "do you think that when we care very much for a person or a thing, we put it into God's place?"

"If you care more for it than you do for Him. Not otherwise."

"How is one to know that?"

"Ask your own heart how you would feel if God demanded it from you."

"How ought I to feel?"

"Sorry, perhaps; but not resentful. Not as though the Lord had no right to ask this at your hands. Grief is allowed; 'tis murmuring that displeases Him."

When Mrs Dorothy said this, Phoebe felt conscious of a dim conviction, buried somewhere very deep down, that there was something which she hoped God would not demand from her. She did not know herself what it was. It was not exactly that she would refuse to give it up; but rather that she hoped she would never be called upon to do it—that if she were it would be a very hard thing to do.

Phoebe left the Maidens' Lodge, and walked slowly across

the Park to White-Ladies. She was feeling for the unknown cause of this sentiment of vague soreness at her heart. She had not found it, when a voice broke in upon her meditations.

"Mrs Latrobe?"

Phoebe came to a sudden stop, and with her heart heating wildly, looked up into the face of Osmund Derwent.

"I am too happy to have met with you," said he. "I was on my way to White-Ladies. May I presume to ask your good offices, Mrs Phoebe, to favour me so far as to present me to Madam Furnival!"

Phoebe courtesied her assent.

"Mrs Rhoda, I trust, is well?"

"She is very well, I thank you."

"I am rejoiced to hear it. You will not, I apprehend, Mrs Phoebe, suffer any surprise, if I tell you of my hopes with regard to Mrs Rhoda. You must, surely, have seen, when at Delawarr Court, what was my ambition. Think you there is any chance for me with Madam Furnival?"

It was well for Osmund Derwent that he had not the faintest idea of what was going on beneath the still, white face of the girl who walked beside him so quietly. She understood now. She knew, revealed as by a flash of lightning, what it was which it would be hard work to resign at God's call.

It was Rhoda for whom he cared—not Phoebe. Phoebe was interesting to him, simply as being in his mind associated with Rhoda. And Rhoda did not want him: and Phoebe had to tell him so.

So she told him. "I am sure Madam would receive you with a welcome," she said. "But as for Mrs Rhoda, 'tis best you should know she stands promised already."

Mr Derwent thought Phoebe particularly unsympathising. People often do think so of those whose "hands are clasped above a hidden pain," and who have to speak with forced calmness, as the only way in which they dare speak at all. He felt a little hurt; he had thought Phoebe so friendly at Delawarr Court.

"To whom?" he asked, almost angrily.

"Mr Marcus Welles."

"That painted fop!" cried Derwent.

Phoebe was silent.

"You really mean that? She is positively promised to him?"

"She is promised to him."

Phoebe spoke in a dull, low, dreamy tone. She felt as though she were in a dream: all these events which were passing around her never could be real. She heard Osmund Derwent's bitter comments, as though she heard them not. She was conscious of only one wish for the future—to be left alone with God.

Osmund Derwent was extremely disappointed in Phoebe. He had expected much more sympathy and consideration from her. He said to himself, in the moments which he could spare from the main subject, that Phoebe did not understand him, and did not feel for him in the least. She had never loved anybody—that was plain!

And meantime, simply to bear and wait, until he chose to leave her, taxed all Phoebe's powers to her uttermost.

She was left alone at last. But instead of going back to the house, where she had no certainty of privacy, Phoebe plunged into the shade of a clump of cedars and cypresses, and sat down at the foot of one of them.

It was a lovely, cloudless day. Through the bright feathery green of a Syrian cypress she looked up into the clear blue sky above. Her love for Osmund Derwent—for she gave it the right name now—was a hopeless thing. His heart was gone from her beyond recall.

"But Thou remainest!"

The words flashed on her, accompanied by the well-remembered tones of her father's voice. She recollected that they had formed the text of the last sermon he had preached. She heard him say again, as he had said to her on his death-bed, "Dear little Phoebe, remember always, there is no way out of any sin or sorrow except Christ." The tears came now. There was relief and healing in them.

"But Thou remainest!"

"Can I suffice for Heaven, and not for earth?"

Phoebe's face showed no sign, when she reached home, of the tempest which had swept over her heart.

"Phoebe, I desire you would wait a moment," said Madam that evening after prayers, when Phoebe, candle in hand, was about to follow Rhoda.

"Yes, Madam." Phoebe put down the candle, and stood waiting.

Madam did not continue till the last of the servants had left the room. Then she said, "Child, I have writ a letter to your mother."

"I thank you, Madam," replied Phoebe.

"And I have sent her ten guineas."

"I thank you very much, Madam."

"I will not disguise from you, my dear, that I cannot but be sensible of the propriety and discretion of your conduct since you came. I think myself obliged to tell you, child, that 'tis on your account I have done so much as this."

"I am sure, Madam, I am infinitely grateful to you."

"And now for another matter. Child, I wish to know your opinion of Mr Edmundson."

"If you please, Madam, I did not like him," said Phoebe, honestly; "nor I think he did not me."

"That would not much matter, my dear," observed Madam, referring to the last clause. "But 'tis a pity you do not like him, for while I would be sorry to force your inclinations, yet you cannot hope to do better."

"If you would allow me to say so, Madam," answered Phoebe, modestly, yet decidedly, "I cannot but think I should do better to be as I am."

Madam shook her head, but did not answer in words. She occupied herself for a little while in settling her mittens to her satisfaction, though she was just going to pull them off. Then she said, "'Tis pity. Well! go to bed, child; we must talk more of it to-morrow. Bid Betty come to me at once, as you pass; I am drowsy to-night."

"I say, Fib," said Rhoda, who had adopted (from Molly) this not very complimentary diminutive for her cousin's name, but only used it when she was in a good humour—"I say, Fib, what did Madam want of you?"

"To know what I thought of Mr Edmundson."

"What fun! Well, what did you?"

"Why, I hoped his sermons would be better than himself: and they weren't."

"Did you tell Madam that?" inquired Rhoda, convulsed with laughter.

"No, not exactly that; I said—"

"O Fib, I wish you had! She thinks it tip-top impertinence in any woman to presume to have an opinion about a sermon. My word! wouldn't you have caught it!"

"Well, I simply told her the truth," replied Phoebe; "that I didn't like him, and I didn't think he liked me."

Rhoda went off into another convulsion.

"O Fib, you are good—nobody better! What did she say to that?"

Emily Sarah Holt

"She said his not fancying me wouldn't signify. But I think it would signify a good deal to me, if I had to be his wife."

"Well, she wouldn't think so, not a bit," said Rhoda, still laughing. "She'd just be thunderstruck if Mr Edmundson, or anybody else in his place, refused the honour of marrying anybody related to her. Shouldn't I like to see him do it! It would take her down a peg, I reckon."

This last elegant expression was caught from Molly.

"Well, I am sure I would rather be refused than taken unwillingly."

"Where did you get your notions. Fib? They are not the mode at all. You were born on the wrong side of fifty, I do think."

"Which is the wrong side of fifty?" suggestively asked Phoebe.

"I wish you wouldn't murder me with laughing," said Rhoda. "Look here now: what shall I be married in?"

"White and silver, Mrs Marcella said, this morning."

("This morning!" Phoebe's words came back no her. Was it only this morning?)

"Thank you! nothing so insipid for me. I think I'll have pink and dove-colour. What do you say?"

"I don't think I would have pink," said Phoebe, mentally comparing that colour with Rhoda's red and white complexion. "Blue would suit you better."

"Well, blue does become me," answered Rhoda, contemplating herself in the glass. "But then, would blue and dove-colour do? I think it should be blue and cold. Or blue and silver? What do you think, Phoebe? I say!"—and suddenly Rhoda turned round and faced Phoebe—"what does Madam mean by having Mr Dawson here? Betty says he was here twice while we were visiting, and he is coming again tomorrow. What can it mean? Is she altering her will, do you suppose?"

"I am sure I don't know, Cousin," said Phoebe.

"I shouldn't wonder if she is. I dare say she'll leave you one or two hundred pounds," said Rhoda, with extreme benignity. "Really, I wish she would. You're a good little thing, Fib, for all your whims."

"Thank you, Cousin," said Phoebe, meekly.

And the cousins went to sleep with amiable feelings towards each other.

The dawn was just creeping over the earth when something awoke Phoebe. Something like the faint tingle of a bell seemed to linger in her ears.

"Rhoda!—did you hear that?" she asked.

"Hear what?" demanded Rhoda, in a very sleepy voice.

"I fancied I heard a bell," said Phoebe, trying to listen.

"Oh, nonsense!" answered Rhoda, rather more awake. "Go to sleep. You've been dreaming."

And Phoebe, accepting the solution, took the advice. She

was scarcely asleep again, as it seemed to her, when the door was softly opened, and Betty came in.

"Mrs Rhoda, my dear, you'd better get up."

"What time is it?" sleepily murmured Rhoda.

"You'd better get up," repeated Betty. "Never mind the time."

"Betty, is there something the matter?"

Betty ignored Phoebe's question.

"Come, my dear, jump up!" she said, still addressing Rhoda. "You'll be wanted by-and-bye."

"Who wants me?" inquired Rhoda, making no effort to rise.

"Well, Mr Dawson, the lawyer, is coming presently, and you'll have to see him."

"I!" Rhoda's eyes opened pretty wide. "Why should I see him? 'Tis Madam wants him, not me."

To the astonishment of both the girls, Betty burst out crying.

"Betty, I am sure something has happened," said Phoebe, springing up. "What is the matter?"

"O, my dear, Madam's gone!" sobbed Betty. "Poor dear gentlewoman! She'll never see anybody again. Mrs Rhoda, she's died in the night."

There was a moment of silent horror, as the eyes of the cousins met. Then Phoebe said under her breath—

"That bell!"

"Yes, poor dear Madam, she rang her bell," said Betty; "but she could not speak when I got to her. I don't think she was above ten minutes after. I've sent off sharp for Dr Saunders, and Mr Dawson too; but 'tis too late—eh, poor dear gentlewoman!"

"Did you send for Mr Leighton?" asked Rhoda, in an awe-struck voice.

"Oh dear, yes, I sent for him too; but la! what can he do?" answered Betty, wiping her eyes.

They all came in due order: Dr Saunders to pronounce that Madam had been dead three hours—"of a cardial malady," said he, in a professionally mysterious manner; Mr Leighton, the Vicar of Tewkesbury, to murmur a few platitudes about the virtues and charity to the poor which had distinguished the deceased lady, and to express his firm conviction that so exalted a character would be at once enrolled among the angelic host, even though she had not been so happy as to receive the Holy Sacrament. Mr Dawson came last, and his concern appeared to be awakened rather for the living than the dead.

"Sad business this!" said he, as he entered the parlour, where the cousins sat, close together, drawn to one another by the fellowship of suffering, in a manner they had never been before. "Sad business! Was to have seen me to-day—important matter. Humph!"

The girls looked at him, but neither spoke.

"Do you know," he pursued, apparently addressing himself to both, "how your grandmother had arranged her affairs?"

Emily Sarah Holt

"No," said Rhoda and Phoebe together.

"Humph! Pity! Been a good deal better for you, my dear young gentlewoman, if she had lived another four-and-twenty hours."

Neither said "Which?" for both thought they knew.

"Poor Phoebe!" said Rhoda, pressing her hand. "But never mind, dear; I'll give it you, just right, what she meant you to have. We'll see about it before I'm married. Oh dear!—that will have to be put off, I suppose."

"You are going to be married?" asked the lawyer.

"Yes," said Rhoda, bridling.

"Humph!—good thing for you."

Mr Dawson marched to the window, with his hands in his pockets, and stood there softly whistling for some seconds.

"Got any money?" he abruptly inquired.

"I? No," said Rhoda.

"No, no; your intended."

"Oh! Yes—three thousand a year."

"Humph!" Mr Dawson whistled again. Then, making as if he meant to leave the room, he suddenly brought up before Phoebe.

"Are *you* going to be married?"

"No, Sir," said Phoebe, blushing.

"Humph!" ejaculated the lawyer, once again.

Silence followed for a few seconds.

"Funeral on Sunday, I suppose? Read the will on Monday morning—eh?"

"Yes, if you please," said Rhoda, who was very much subdued.

"Good. Well!—good morning! Poor girl!" The last words were in an undertone.

"I am so sorry for it, Phoebe, dear," said Rhoda, who was always at her best under the pressure of trial. "But never you mind—you shall have it. I'll make it up to you."

Rhoda now naturally assumed the responsibility of mistress, and gave orders that no visitor should be admitted excepting the Vicar and Mr Welles. The evening brought the latter gentleman, who had apparently spent the interval in arraying himself in faultless mourning.

"I am so grieved, my charmer!" exclaimed Mr Marcus Welles, dropping on one knee, and lifting Rhoda's hand to his lips. "Words cannot paint my distress on hearing of your sorrow. Had I been a bird, I would have flown to offer you consolation. Pray do not dim your bright eyes, my fair. 'Tis but what happens to all, and specially in old age. Old folks must die, you know, dearest Madam; and, after all, did they not, young folks would find them very often troublesome. But you have now no one over you, and you see your slave at your feet."

Emily Sarah Holt

And with a most unexceptionable bow, Mr Marcus gently possessed himself of Rhoda's fan, wherewith he began fanning her in the most approved manner. It occurred to Phoebe that if the gentleman's grief had been really genuine, it was doubtful whether his periods would have been quite so polished. Rhoda's sorrow, while it might prove evanescent, was honest while it lasted: and had been much increased by the extreme suddenness of the calamity.

"I thank you, Sir," she said quietly. "And I am sure you will be grieved to hear that my grandmother died just too soon to make that provision she intended for my cousin. So the lawyer has told us this morning. You will not, I cannot but think, oppose my wish to give her what it was meant that she should have."

"Dearest Madam!" and Mr Welles' hand went to his heart, "you cannot have so little confidence in me as to account it possible that I could oppose any wish of yours!"

Engaged persons did not, at that time, call each other by the Christian name. It would have been considered indecorous.

"I was sure, Sir, you would say no less," answered Rhoda.

CHAPTER TEN

MR. WELLES DOES IT BEAUTIFULLY

"Thy virtues lost, thou would'st not look
Me in thy chains to hold?
Know, friend, thou verily hast lost
Thy chiefest virtue—gold."

Nine o'clock on the Monday morning was the hour appointed for reading Madam's will. When Rhoda and Phoebe, in their deep mourning, entered the parlour, they were startled to find the number of persons already assembled. Not only all the household and outdoor servants, but all the inmates of the Maidens' Lodge, excepting Mrs Marcella, and several others, stood up to receive the young ladies as they passed on to the place reserved for them.

Mr Dawson handed the girls to their places, and then seated himself at the table, and proceeded to unfold a large parchment.

"It will be well that I should remark," said he, looking up over his spectacles, "that the late Madam Furnival had intended, at the time of her death, to execute a fresh will. I am sorry to say it was not signed. This, therefore, is her last will, as duly executed. It bears date the fourteenth of

Emily Sarah Holt

November, in the year 1691—"

An ejaculation of dismay, though under her breath, came from Rhoda, the lawyer went on:—

"—When Mrs Catherine Peveril, mother of Mrs Rhoda here, was just married, and before the marriage of Mrs Anne Furnival, mother to Mrs Phoebe Latrobe, who is also present. The intended will would have made provision for both of these young gentlewomen, grand-daughters to Madam Furnival. By the provisions of the present one, one of them is worsened, and the other bettered."

Rhoda's alarm was over. The last sentence reassured her.

Mr Dawson cleared his voice, and began to read. The will commenced with the preamble then usual, in which the testatrix declared her religious views as a member of the Church of England; and went on to state that she wished to be buried with her ancestors, in the family vault, in the nave of Tewkesbury Abbey. One hundred pounds was bequeathed to the Vicar of Tewkesbury, for the time being; twenty pounds and a suit of mourning to every servant who should have been in her employ for five years at the date of her death; six months' wages to those who should have been with her for a shorter time; a piece of black satin sufficient to make a gown, mantua, and hood, and forty pounds in money, to each inmate of the Maidens' Lodge. Mourning rings were left to the Maidens, the Vicar. Dr Saunders, Mr Dawson, and several friends mentioned by name, of whom Sir Richard Delawarr was one. Then the testatrix gave, devised, and bequeathed to her "dear daughter Catherine, wife of Francis Peveril, Esquire, with remainder to the heirs of her body, the sum of two thousand pounds of lawful money."

Rhoda's face grew eager, as she listened for the

next sentence.

"Lastly, I give, devise, and bequeath the Abbey of Cressingham, commonly called White-Ladies, and all other my real and personal estate whatsoever, not hereinbefore excepted, to my dear daughter Anne Furnival, her heirs, assigns, administrators, and executors for ever."

The effect was crushing. That one sentence had changed everything. Not Rhoda, but Phoebe, was the heiress of White-Ladies.

Mr Dawson calmly finished reading the signatures and attestation clause, and then folded up the will, and once more looked over his spectacles.

"Mrs Phoebe, as your mother's representative, give me leave to wish you joy. Shall you wish to write to her? I must, of course. The letters could go together."

Phoebe looked up, half-bewildered.

"I scarcely understand," she said. "There is something left to Mother, is there not?"

"My dear young gentlewoman, there is everything left to her. She is the lady of the manor."

"Just what is there for Rhoda?" gasped Phoebe, apparently not at all elated by her change of position.

"A poor, beggarly two thousand pounds!" burst out Rhoda. "'Tis a shame! And I always thought I was to have White-Ladies! I shall just be nobody now! Nobody will respect me, and I can never cut any figure. Well! I'm glad I am engaged to be married. That's safe, at any rate."

The elevation of Mr Dawson's eyebrows, and the pursing of his lips, might have implied a query on that score.

"I'm so sorry, dear!" said Phoebe, gently. "For you, of course, I mean. I could not be sorry that there was something for Mother, because she is not well off; but I am very sorry you are disappointed."

"You can't help it!" was Rhoda's rather repelling answer. Still, through all her anger, she remembered to be just.

"Certainly not, my dear Mrs Phoebe," said the lawyer. "'Tis nobody's fault—not even Madam Furnival's, for the new will would have given White-Ladies to Mrs Rhoda, and five thousand pounds to Mrs Anne Latrobe. Undoubtedly she intended, Mrs Rhoda, you should have it."

"Then why can't I?" demanded Rhoda, fiercely.

Mr Dawson shook his head, with a pitying smile. "The law knows nothing of intentions," said he: "only of deeds fully performed. Still, it may be a comfort in your disappointment, to remember that this was meant for you."

"Thank you for your comfort!" said Rhoda, bitterly. "Why, it makes it all the worse."

"I wish—" but Phoebe stopped short.

"Oh, I don't blame you," said Rhoda, impetuously. "'Tis no fault of yours. If she'd done it now, lately, I might have thought so. But a will that was made before either you or me was born—" Rhoda's grammar always suffered from her excitement—"can't be your fault, nor anybody else's. But 'tis a shame, for all that. She'd no business to let me go on all these years, expecting to have everything, and knew all the while her will wasn't right made. 'Tis too bad! My Lady Betty!—Mrs Dorothy!—don't you think so?"

"My dear," said Lady Betty, "I am indeed grieved for your disappointment. But there is decorum, my dear Mrs Rhoda—there is decorum!"

"No, my dear," was Mrs Dorothy's answer. "I dare not call anything bad that the Lord doth. Had it been His will you should have White-Ladies, be sure you would have had it."

"Well, you know," said Rhoda, in a subdued tone, and folding one of her black gauze ribbons into minute plaits, "of course, one can't complain of God."

"Ah, child!" sighed Mrs Dorothy, "I wish one could not!"

"O my dear Mrs Rhoda, I feel for you so dreadfully!" accompanied the tragically clasped hands of Mrs Clarissa. "My feelings are so keen, and run away with me so—"

"Then let 'em!" said Mrs Jane Talbot's voice behind. "Mine won't. My dears, I'm sorry you've lost Madam. But as to the money and that, I'll wait ten years, and then I'll tell you which I'm sorry for."

"Well, I'm sorry for both of you," added Mrs Eleanor Darcy. "I don't think, Mrs Phoebe, my dear, you'll lie on roses."

No one was more certain of that than Phoebe herself.

She wrote a few lines to her mother, which went inside Mr Dawson's letter. Mrs Latrobe was in service near Reading. Her daughter felt sure that she would lose no time in taking possession. The event proved that she was right. The special messenger whom Mr Dawson sent with the letters returned

Emily Sarah Holt

with an answer to each. Phoebe's mother wrote to her thus:—

"Child,—Mr Dawson hath advertized me of the deth of Madam Furnivall, my mother. I would have you, on rect of this, to lett your cousen know that shee need not lieve the house afore I come, wich will be as soon as euer I can winde all upp and bee wth you. I would like to make aquaintance wth her ere anything be settled. I here from the layer [by which Mrs Latrobe meant *lawyer*] that she is to be maried, and it will be soe much ye better for you. I trust you may now make a good match yrself. But I shal see to all yt when I com.

"Yr mother, A. Latrobe."

Phoebe studied every word of this letter, and the more she studied it, the less she liked it. First, it looked as if Mrs Latrobe did mean Rhoda to leave the house, though she graciously intimated her intention of making acquaintance with her before she did so. Secondly, she was evidently in a hurry to come. Thirdly, she congratulated herself on Rhoda's approaching marriage, because it would get rid of her, and leave the way open for Phoebe. And lastly, she threatened Phoebe with "a good match." Phoebe thought, with a sigh, that "the time was out of joint," and heartily wished that the stars would go back into their courses.

Mrs Latrobe managed to wind all up in a surprisingly short time. She reached her early home in the cool of a summer evening, Rhoda having sent the family coach to meet her at Tewkesbury. Phoebe had said nothing to her cousin of any approaching change, which she thought it best to leave to her mother; so she contented herself by saying that Mrs Latrobe wished to make the acquaintance of her niece. Lady Betty kindly came up to help the inexperienced girls in making due preparation for the arrival of the lady of the manor. When the coach rolled up to the front door, Phoebe was standing on the steps, Lady Betty and Rhoda further back in the hall.

Mrs Latrobe was attired in new and stylish mourning.

"Ah, child, here you are!" was her first greeting to Phoebe. "The old place is grown greyer. Those trees come too near the windows; I shall cut some of them down. Where is your cousin?"

Rhoda heard the inquiry, and she stepped forward.

"Let us look at you, child," said Mrs Latrobe, turning to her. "Ah, you are like Kitty—not so good-looking, though."

"Mother," said Phoebe, gently, "this is my Lady Betty Morehurst. She was so kind as to help us in getting ready for you."

Mrs Latrobe appraised Lady Betty by means of one rapid glance. Then she thanked her with an amount of effulgence which betrayed either subservience or contempt. Lady Betty received her thanks with a quiet dignity which refused to be ruffled, kissed Rhoda and Phoebe, and took her leave, declining to remain even for the customary dish of tea. Mrs Latrobe drew off her gloves, sat down in Madam's cushioned chair, and desired Phoebe to give her some tea.

"Let me see, child!" she said, looking at Rhoda. "You are near one-and-twenty, I suppose?"

Rhoda admitted the fact.

"And what do you think of doing?"

Rhoda looked blankly first at her aunt, then at her cousin.

Emily Sarah Holt

Phoebe came hastily to the rescue.

"She is shortly to be married, Mother; did you forget?"

"Ah!" said Mrs Latrobe, still contemplating Rhoda. "Well—if it hold—you may as well be married from hence, I suppose. Is the day fixed?"

"No, Aunt Anne."

"I think, my dear," remarked Mrs Latrobe, sipping her tea, "'twould be better if you said Madam.—Why, Phoebe, what old-fashioned china! Sure it cannot have been new these forty years. I shall sweep away all that rubbish.—Whom are you going to marry? Is he well off?—Phoebe, those shoe-buckles of yours are quite shabby. I cannot have you wear such trumpery. You must remember what is due to you.—Well, my dear?"

Rhoda had much less practice in the school of patience than Phoebe, and she found the virtue difficult just then. But she restrained herself as well as she could.

"I am engaged in marriage with Mr Marcus Welles; and he has an estate, and spends three thousand pounds by the year."

"Welles! A Welles of Buckinghamshire?"

"His estate is in this shire," said Rhoda.

"Three thousand! That's not much. Could you have done no better? He expected you would have White-Ladies, I suppose?"

"I suppose so. I did," said Rhoda, shortly.

"My dear, you have some bad habits," said Mrs Latrobe, "which Phoebe should have broken you of before I came. 'Tis very rude to answer without giving a name."

"You told me not to give you one, Aunt Anne."

"You are slow at catching meanings, my dear," replied Mrs Latrobe, with that calm nonchalance so provoking to an angry person. "I desired you to call me Madam, as 'tis proper you should."

"Phoebe doesn't," burst from Rhoda.

"Then she ought," answered Mrs Latrobe, coolly examining the crest on a tea-spoon.

"Oh, I will, Rhoda, if Mother wishes it," put in Phoebe, anxious above all things to keep the peace.

Rhoda vouchsafed no reply to either.

"Well!" said the lady of the manor, rising, "you will carry me to my chamber, child," addressing Rhoda. "You can stay here, Phoebe. Your cousin will wait on me."

It was something new for Rhoda to wait on anyone. She swallowed her pride with the best grace she could, and turned to open the door.

"I suppose you have had the best room made ready for me?" inquired Mrs Latrobe, as she passed out.

"Madam's chamber," replied Rhoda.

"Oh, but—not the one in which she died?"

"Yes," answered Rhoda; adding, after a momentary struggle with herself, "Madam."

"Oh, but that will never do!" said Mrs Latrobe, hastily. "I couldn't sleep there! A room in which someone died scarce a month ago! Where is my woman? Call her. I must have that changed."

Rhoda summoned Betty, who came, courtesying. Her mistress was too much preoccupied in mind to notice the civility.

"Why, what could you all be thinking of, to put me in this chamber? I must have another. This is the best, I know; but I cannot think of sleeping here. Show me the next best—that long one in the south wing."

"That is the young gentlewomen's chamber, Madam," objected Betty.

"Well, what does that matter?" demanded Mrs Latrobe, sharply. "Can't they have another? I suppose I come first!"

"Yes, of course, Madam," said subdued Betty.

Rhoda looked dismayed, but kept silence. She was learning her lesson. Mrs Latrobe looked into the girls' room, rapidly decided on it, and ordered it to be got ready for her.

"Then which must the young gentlewomen have, Madam?" inquired Betty.

"Oh, any," said Mrs Latrobe, carelessly. "There are enough."

"Which would you like, Mrs Rhoda?" incautiously asked Betty.

Before Rhoda could reply, her aunt said quickly,—

"Ask Mrs Phoebe, if you please."

And Betty remembered that the cousins had changed places. It was a very bitter pill to Rhoda; and it was not like Rhoda to say—yet she said it, as soon as she had the opportunity—

"Phoebe, Aunt Anne means you to choose our room: please don't have a little stuffy one."

"Dear Rhoda, which would you like?" responded Phoebe at once.

A little sob escaped Rhoda.

"Oh, Phoebe, you are going to be the only one who is good to me! I should like that other long one in the north wing, that matches ours; but don't choose it if you don't like it."

"We will have that," said Phoebe, reassuringly; "at least, if Mother leaves it to me."

Thus early it was made evident that the old nature in Anne Latrobe was scotched, not killed. Sorrow seemed to have laid merely a repressive hand upon her bad qualities, and to have uprooted none but good ones. The brilliance and playfulness of her early days were gone. The *coeur leger* had turned to careless self-love, the impetuosity had become peevish obstinacy.

"Old Madam never spoke to me in that way!" said Betty. "She liked to have her way, poor dear gentlewoman, as well as anybody; and she wouldn't take a bit of impudence like so much barley-sugar, I'll not say she would; but she was a gentlewoman, every inch of her, that she was. And that's

Emily Sarah Holt

more than you can say for some folks!"

The next morning, all the Maidens—the invalid, as usual, excepted—came trooping up one after another, to pay their respects to the new lady of the manor.

Lady Betty came first; then Mrs Dorothy and Mrs Eleanor, together; after a little while, Mrs Clarissa; and lastly, Mrs Jane.

"My dear Mrs Anne, I remember you well, though perhaps you can scarce recollect me," said Mrs Dorothy, "for you were but nine years old the last time that I saw you. May the Lord bless you, my dear, and make you a blessing!"

"Oh, I don't doubt I shall do my duty," was the response of Mrs Latrobe, which very much satisfied herself and greatly dissatisfied Mrs Dorothy.

"'Tis delightful to see you back, dear Madam Latrobe!" said Mrs Clarissa, gushingly. "How touching must it be to return to the home of your youth, after so many years of banishment!"

Mrs Latrobe had not felt in the least touched, and hardly knew how to reply. "Oh, to be sure!" she said. "Glad to see you," said Mrs Jane. "Great loss we've had in Madam. Hope you'll be as good as she was. My sister desired me to make her compliments. Can't stir off the sofa. Fine morning!"

When the Maidens left the Abbey—which they did together —they compared notes on the new reign.

Lady Betty's sense of decorum was very much shocked. Mrs Latrobe had not spoken a word of her late mother, and had hinted at changes in matters which had existed at

White-Ladies from time immemorial.

Mrs Clarissa was charmed with the new lady's manners and mourning, both which she thought faultless.

Mrs Eleanor thought "she was a bit shy, poor thing! We must make allowances, my dear friends—we must make allowances!"

"Make fiddlestrings!" growled Mrs Jane. "She's Anne Furnival still, and she'll be Anne Furnival to the end of the chapter. As if I didn't know Nancy! Ever drive a jibbing horse?"

Mrs Clarissa, who was thus suddenly appealed to, declared in a shocked tone that she never drove a horse of any description since she was born.

"Ah, well! I have," resumed Mrs Jane, ignoring the scandalised tone of her sister Maiden: "and that's just Nancy Furnival. She's as sleek in the coat as ever a Barbary mare. But you'll not get her along the road to Tewkesbury, without you make her think you want to drive her to Gloucester. I heard plenty of folks pitying Madam when she bolted. My word!—but I pitied somebody else a vast deal more, and that was Charles Latrobe. I wouldn't have married her, if she'd been stuck all over with diamonds."

"I fancy she drove him," said Mrs Eleanor with a smile.

"Like enough, poor soul!" responded Mrs Jane. "Only chance he had of any peace. He was a decent fellow enough, too,—if only he had kept clear of Nancy."

"What made him marry her?" thoughtfully asked Mrs Eleanor.

"Deary me!" exclaimed Mrs Jane. "When did you ever see a man that could fathom a woman? Good, simple soul that he was!—she made him think black was white with holding up a finger. She glistened bravely, and he thought she was gold. Well!—*we* shan't have much peace now,—take my word for it. Eh, this world!—'tis a queer place as ever I saw."

"True, my dear," replied Mrs Dorothy: "let us therefore be thankful there is a better."

But her opinion of Mrs Latrobe was not given.

The same evening, as Phoebe sat in the parlour with her mother, Betty came in with a courtesy.

"Mr Marcus Welles, to speak with Madam."

"With Mrs Rhoda?" asked Phoebe, rising. "I will go seek her."

"No, if you please, Mrs Phoebe: Mr Welles said, Madam or yourself."

"Phoebe, my dear, do not be such a fid-fad!" entreated Mrs Latrobe. "If Rhoda is wanted, she can be sought.—Good evening, Sir! I am truly delighted to have the pleasure of seeing you, and I trust we shall be better acquainted."

Mr Welles bowed low over Mrs Latrobe's extended hand.

"Madam, the delight is mine, and the honour. Mrs Phoebe, your servant,—your most humble servant."

It was the first time that Mr Welles had ever addressed Phoebe with more than a careless "good evening."

"Ready to serve you, Sir," said she, courtesying. "Shall I seek my cousin? She has wanted your company, I think."

This was a very audacious speech for Phoebe: but she thought it so extraordinary that Mr Welles had not paid one visit to his betrothed since the funeral, that she took the liberty of reminding him of it.

"Madam," said Mr Welles, with a complacent smile, toying with his gold chatelaine, "I really could not have visited you sooner, under the circumstances in which I found myself."

"Phoebe! have you lost your senses?" inquired Mrs Latrobe, sharply.

"I am sure," resumed Mr Marcus Welles, with an extremely graceful wave of his hand towards Mrs Latrobe, "that Madam will fully enter into my much lacerated feelings, and see how very distressing 'twould have been both to myself and her, had I forced my company on Mrs Rhoda, as matters stand at present."

Phoebe sat listening with a face of utter bewilderment. By what means had Mr Welles' feelings been lacerated?—and why should it be more distressing for him to meet Rhoda now than before?—But she kept silence, and Mrs Latrobe said,—

"I think, Sir, I have the honour to understand you."

"Madam!" replied Mr Marcus Welles, with his courtliest bow, "I am sure that a gentlewoman of your parts and discretion can do no less, I cannot but be infinitely sensible of the severe and cruel loss I am about to sustain: still, to my small estate, any other dealing would be of such mischievous consequence, that I think myself obliged to resign the views I

Emily Sarah Holt

proposed to myself."

Phoebe tried to understand him, and found it impossible.

"This being the case," continued he, "you will understand, dear Madam, that I thought myself engaged to wait until I might be honoured by some discourse with you: and meanwhile to abstain from any commerce of discourse in other quarters, till I had permission to acquaint you of the affair. I have indeed been in pain until I was able to wait upon you. I shall now be something eased. You, I am certain, dearest Madam, will contrive the business far better than my disordered mind would allow me; and I doubt not 'twould be more agreeable to all parties to communicate by that canal."

"If you wish it, Sir, it shall certainly be so," answered Mrs Latrobe, who seemed to be under no doubt concerning Mr Welles' meaning. "I am yours to serve you in the matter."

"Dearest Madam, you are an angel of mercy! The sooner I retire, then, the better."

He kissed Mrs Latrobe's hand, and came round to Phoebe.

"Mr Welles, you have not seen Rhoda yet. I do not understand!" said Phoebe blankly, as he bowed iver her hand.

"Madam, I have but just now engaged myself—"

"Phoebe, don't be a goose!" burst from her mother. "You must be a baby if you do not understand. Cannot you see that Mr Welles, in a most honourable manner, which does him infinite credit, withdraws all pretensions to your cousin's hand, leaving her free to engage herself elsewhere? Really, I should have thought you had sense enough for that."

For a moment Phoebe looked, with a bewildered air, from her mother to Mr Welles. Then shyness, fear and reserve gave way before indignation. She did understand now.

"You mean to desert Rhoda, because she has lost the paltry money that you expected she would have?"

For once in his life, Mr Marcus Welles seemed startled and taken at a disadvantage.

"I was afraid you wanted her chiefly for her money, but I did not believe you capable of this! So you do not care for her at all? And you run away, afraid to face the pangs you have created, and to meet the eyes of the maid you have so foully wronged. Shame on you!"

"Phoebe, you must be mad!" exclaimed Mrs Latrobe, rising. "Don't listen to her, dear Mr Welles; 'tis a most distressing scene for you to bear. I am infinitely concerned my daughter should have so far forgotten herself as to address you with such vulgar abuse. I can only excuse her on the ground—"

"Dearest Madam, there is every excuse," said Mr Welles, with the sweetest magnanimity. "Sweet Mrs Phoebe is a woodland bird, untrammelled as yet by those fetters which we men and women of the world must needs bear. 'Tis truly delightful to see the charming generosity and the admirable fire with which she plays the knight-errant. Indeed, Madam, such disinterested warmth and fervour of heart are seen but too seldom in this worn old world. Suffer me to entreat you not to chide Mrs Phoebe for her charming simplicity and high spirit."

"Since Mr Welles condescends to intercede for you, Phoebe, notwithstanding your shocking behaviour, I am willing to overlook it this time; but I warn you I shall not prove thus easy another time."

"I am sure I hope there will never be another time!" cried Phoebe, her eyes flashing.

"Phoebe, go to your chamber, and don't let me hear one word more," said Mrs Latrobe, severely.

And Phoebe obeyed, rushing upstairs with feet that seemed to keep pace with the whirlwind in her heart.

"Phoebe, I wonder whether of these ribbons, the silk or the gauze, would go best with—Why, whatever in the world is the matter?" said Rhoda, breaking off.

"You may well ask, my dear," answered the voice of Mrs Latrobe, behind Phoebe. "Your cousin has been conducting herself in a most improper manner—offering gross insults to my guests in my house."

"Phoebe!" cried Rhoda, as if she could not believe her ears.

"Yes, Phoebe. She really has. I can only fear—indeed, I had almost said hope—that her wits are something impaired. What think you of her telling a gentleman who had acted in a most noble and honourable manner—exactly as a gentleman should do—that she could not have believed him capable of such baseness? and she cried shame on him!"

"Not Phoebe!" exclaimed Rhoda again, looking from one to the other very much as Phoebe had done. "Why, Phoebe, what does all this mean?"

"Oh, Rhoda, I can't tell you!" said Phoebe, sobbing, for the reaction had come. "Mother, you will have to tell her. I can't."

"Of course I shall tell her," calmly answered Mrs Latrobe. "I came for that very thing. Rhoda, my dear, I am sure you are a maid of sense and discretion."

"I hope so, Madam."

"So do I, child: and therefore you will hear me calmly, and not fly into passions like that silly maid yonder. My dear, you must have remembered, I am certain, that when you promised yourself to Mr Welles, you were in a very different situation from now."

Rhoda only bowed. Perhaps, on that subject, she was afraid to trust her voice.

"And, of course, it has also occurred to you, my dear, that this being the case, you could not in honour hold Mr Welles bound to you any longer, if he wished to be free?"

"But we don't wish to be free," said Rhoda, in a puzzled tone.

"You are mistaken, my dear, so far as one of you is concerned. Perhaps it had been yet more graceful had you been the one to loose the bond: yet Mr Welles has done it with so infinite a grace and spirit that I can scarce regret your omission. My dear, you are now entirely free. He sets you completely at liberty, and has retired from all pretension to you."

"But what, Aunt Anne—I do not understand you!" exclaimed Rhoda, in accents of bewildered amazement, which had a ring of agony beneath, as though she was struggling against the comprehension of a grief she was reluctant to face.

"Surely, my dear, you must have understood me," said Mrs Latrobe. "Mr Welles resigns his suit to you."

"He has given me up?" bursts from Rhoda's lips.

"He has entirely given you up. You cannot have really expected anything else?"

"I thought *he* was true!" said Rhoda through her set teeth. "Are you sure you understood him? Phoebe, you tell me,—did he mean that?"

"O Rhoda! poor Rhoda! I am afraid he did!" said Phoebe, as distinctly as tears would let her.

"But, my dear," interposed Mrs Latrobe, remonstratingly, "surely you cannot be surprised? When Mr Welles engaged himself to you, it was (as he thought) to the heiress of a large estate. You could not expect him to encumber himself with a wife who brought him less than one year's income of his own. 'Tis not reasonable, child. No man in his senses would do such a thing. We live in the world, my dear,—not in Utopia."

"We live in a hard, cold, wicked, miserable world, and the sooner we are out of it the better!" came in a constrained voice from Rhoda.

"I beg, my dear," answered Mrs Latrobe, "you will not make extravagant speeches. There might be not another man in the world, that you should go into such a frenzy. We shall yet find you a husband, never fear."

"Not one like him, I hope!" murmured Phoebe. "And I don't think Rhoda wants anybody else."

"Phoebe," said her mother, "I am extreme concerned at the coarseness of your speeches. I had hoped you were a gentlewoman."

"Well, Mother," said Phoebe, firing up again, "if Mr Welles be a gentleman, I almost hope not!"

"My dear," said Mrs Latrobe, "Mr Welles is a gentleman. The style in which he announced his desire to withdraw from his suit to your cousin, was perfect. A prince could not have done it better."

"I should hope a prince would not have done it at all!" was the blunt response from Phoebe.

"You are not a woman of the world, my dear, but a very foolish, ignorant child, that does not know properly what she is saying. 'Tis so near bed-time you need not descend again. You will get over your disappointment, Rhoda, when you have slept, and I shall talk with you presently. Good-night, my dears."

And Mrs Latrobe closed the door, and left the cousins together.

CHAPTER ELEVEN

PHOEBE IN A NEW CHARACTER

"We mend broken china, torn lace we repair;
But we sell broken hearts cheap in Vanity Fair."

"Did *she* ever love anybody?" came in a low voice from
Rhoda, when Mrs Latrobe had withdrawn, "Oh, I don't
know!" sobbed Phoebe, who was crying violently, and might
have seemed to a surface observer the more unhappy of the
two.

"Don't weep so," said Rhoda. "I'm sure you don't need. Aunt
Anne will never be angry long—she does not care enough
about anything to keep it up."

"Oh, it is not for myself, Rhoda—poor Rhoda!"

"For me? Surely not, Phoebe. I have never been so good to
you as to warrant that."

"I don't know whether you have been good to me or you
have not, Cousin; but I am so sorry for you!"

Phoebe was kneeling beside the bed. Rhoda came over to
her, and kissed her forehead, and said—what was very much

for Rhoda to say—"I scarce think I deserve you should weep for me, Phoebe."

"But I can't help it!" said Phoebe.

"Well! I reckon I should have known it," said Rhoda, in a rather hard tone. "I suppose that is what all men are like. But I did think he was true—I did!"

"I never did," responded Phoebe.

"Well!" sighed Rhoda again. "Let it pass. Perhaps Mrs Dorothy is right—'tis best to trust none of them."

"I don't think Mrs Dorothy said that," replied Phoebe, heaving a long sigh, as she sat up and pushed back her ruffled hair. "I do hope I wasn't rude to Mother."

"Nothing she'll care about," said Rhoda. "I wondered he did not come, Phoebe."

"So did I, and I told him as much. But—Rhoda, I think perhaps we shall forgive him sooner if we don't talk about it."

"Ah! I have not come to forgiving yet," was Rhoda's answer. "Perhaps I shall some time. Well! I shall be an old maid now, Phoebe, like Mrs Dorothy, I suppose you'll be the one to marry."

"Thank you, I'd rather not!" said Phoebe, quickly. "I am not sure I should like it at all; and I am quite sure I don't want to be married for my money, or for what people expect me to have."

"Oh, there's nothing else in this world!" answered Rhoda,

Emily Sarah Holt

with an air of immense experience. "Don't you expect it. Every man you come across is an avaricious, designing creature. Oh dear! 'tis a weary weary world, and 'tis no good living!"

"Yes, Rhoda dear, there is one good in living, and 'tis always left to us, whatever we may lose," said Phoebe, earnestly. "Don't you remember what the Lord Jesus said to His disciples—'My meat is to do the will of Him that sent Me?' There is always that, Rhoda."

"Ah, that is something I don't know anything about," said Rhoda, wearily. "And I always think 'tis right down shabby of people to turn religious, just because they have lost the world, and are disappointed and tired. And I was never cut out for a saint, Phoebe—'tis no use!"

"Rhoda, dear, when people give all their days to Satan, and then turn religious, as you say, just at last, when they are going to die, or think they are—don't you think that right down shabby? The longer you keep away from God, the less you have to give Him when you come. And as—"

"I thought you Puritans always said we hadn't anything to give to God, but He gave everything to us," objected Rhoda, pettishly.

Phoebe passed the tone by, and answered the words, "I think there are two things we can give to God, Cousin: our sins, that He may cast them into the depths of the sea; and ourselves, that He may save and train us. And the longer you stay away, the more sin you will have to bring; and the less time there will be for loving and serving Him. You will be sorry, when you do come, that you were not sooner."

"How do you know I shall? I tell you, I wasn't cut out for

a saint."

"I think you will, Cousin, because I have asked Him to bring you," said Phoebe, simply; "and it must be His will to hear that; because He willeth not the death of a sinner."

"So you count me a sinner! I am sure I'm very much obliged to you!" said Rhoda, more in her old style than before.

"Yes, dear Cousin, I count you a sinner; and so do I myself, and every body else," said Phoebe, gently.

"Oh, well, I suppose we are all sinners," admitted Rhoda. "Don't I keep telling you I am not made for a saint?"

"But you were, Rhoda; God made you for Himself," said Phoebe.

"Oh, well 'tis no use talking!" and Rhoda got up, and began to pull down her elaborately-dressed hair, with hasty, uncareful fingers. "We'd better go to bed."

"Perhaps it isn't much use talking," said Phoebe, as she rose to help her. "But it is sure to be some praying, so I shall go on."

It was a few days later, and Phoebe was crossing the Park on her way to the Maidens' Lodge, carrying a basket of fruit sent by Mrs Latrobe to Lady Betty. From all the Maidens, except Lady Betty, Mrs Latrobe held aloof. Mrs Jane was too sharp for her, Mrs Marcella too querulous, and Mrs Dorothy too dull. Mrs Clarissa she denounced as "poor vain flirt that could not see her time was passed," and Mrs Eleanor, she declared, gave her the horrors only to look at. But Lady Betty she diligently cultivated. How much of her regard was due to her Ladyship's title, Mrs Latrobe did not explain.

Emily Sarah Holt

Phoebe was nearing the Maidens' Lodge, and had just entered the last glade on her way thither, when—very much to her disapprobation and dismay—from a belt of trees on her left hand, Mr Marcus Welles stepped out and stood before her.

"Your most humble servant, Mrs Phoebe! I was very desirous to have the honour of waiting on you this fine morning; and thinking that I saw you at a little distance, I took the great liberty of accosting you."

If Phoebe had said just what she thought, she would have informed Mr Welles that he had taken a wholly unwarrantable liberty in so doing; for while she sagely counselled Rhoda to forgive the offender, she had by no means forgiven him herself. But being mindful of conventionalities, Phoebe courtesied stiffly, and left Mr Welles to explain himself at his leisure. Now, Mr Welles had come to that glade in the Park for the special purpose of making a communication, which he felt rather an awkward one to make with that amount of grace which beseemed him: nevertheless, being a very adroit young man, and much given to turning corners in a rapid and elegant manner, he determined to go through with the matter. If it had only been anyone but Phoebe!

"Mrs Phoebe," he began, "I cannot but flatter myself that you are not wholly ignorant of the high esteem I have long had for your deep merit."

"Cannot you, Sir?" responded Phoebe, by no means in a promising manner.

Mr Welles felt the manner. He thought his web was scarcely fine-spun enough. He must begin again.

"I trust that Madam is in good health, Mrs Phoebe?"

"My mother is very well, I thank you, Sir."

"You are yourself in good health, I venture to hope, Madam?"

"I am, Sir, I thank you."

The task which Mr Welles had set himself, as he perceived with chagrin, was proving harder than he had anticipated. Phoebe evidently intended to waste no more time on him than she could help.

"The state of affairs at White-Ladies is of infinite concern to me, Madam."

"Is it, Sir?"

"Undoubtedly, Madam. Your health and happiness—all of you—are extreme dear to me."

"Really, Sir!"

"Especially *yours*, Madam."

Phoebe made no answer to this. Her silence encouraged Mr Welles to proceed. He thought his tactics had succeeded, and the creature was coming round by degrees. The only point now requiring care was not to startle her away again.

"Allow me to assure you, Madam, that your welfare is in my eyes a matter of infinite concern."

"So you said, Sir," was Phoebe's cool reply, Mr Welles was very uncomfortable. Had he made any mistake? Was it possible that, after all, the creature was not coming round in an orthodox manner?

"Madam, give me leave to assure you, moreover, that I am infinitely attached to you, and desire no higher happiness than to be permitted to offer you my service."

It was an instant before Phoebe recognised that Mr Marcus Welles was actually making her an offer. When she did, her answer was immediate and unmistakable.

"Don't you, Mr Welles?" said Phoebe. "Then I do!"

"Madam, have you misapprehended me?" demanded her suitor, to whom the idea of any woman refusing him was an impossibility not to be entertained for a moment.

"I should be glad if I had," said Phoebe.

"You must be labouring under some mistake, Madam. I have an estate which brings me in three thousand a year, and I am my own master. 'Tis not an opportunity a maid can look to meet with every day, nor is it every gentlewoman that I would ask to be my wife."

"No—only a golden one!" said Phoebe.

"Madam!"

Phoebe turned, and their eyes met.

"Mr Welles, give me leave to tell you the truth: you do not hear it often. You do not wish to marry me. You wish to obtain White-Ladies. 'Tis of no consequence to you whether the woman that must needs come with it be Phoebe Latrobe or Rhoda Peveril. My cousin would please you better than I; but you really care not a straw for either of us. You only want the estate. Allow me in my turn to assure you that, so far as I am concerned, you will not get it. The man who could use my cousin as you have done may keep away from endeavouring my favour. I wish you a very good morning, Mr Welles."

"I beg, Madam, that you will permit me to explain—" stammered Mr Welles, whose grace and tactics alike forsook him under the treatment to which he was subjected by Phoebe.

"Sir, there is nothing to explain."

And with a courtesy which could be construed into nothing but final dismissal, Phoebe left her astonished suitor to stand and look after her with the air of a beaten general, while she turned the corner of the Maidens' Lodge, and made her way to Lady Betty's door.

Lady Betty was at that moment giving an "at home" on the very minute scale permitted by the diminutive appointments of the Maidens' Lodge. Mrs Jane Talbot and Mrs Dorothy Jennings were seated at her little tea-table.

"Why, my dear Mrs Phoebe! what an unlooked-for pleasure!" exclaimed Lady Betty, coming forward cordially.

If her cordiality had been a shade more distinct since Phoebe became heiress of Cressingham—well, she was only human. The other ladies present had sustained no such change.

"The Lord bless thee, dear child!" was the warm greeting of Mrs Dolly; but it had been quite as warm long before.

"Evening!" said Mrs Jane, with a sarcastic grin. "Got it over, has he? Saw you through the side window. Bless you, child, I know all about it—I expected that all along. Hope you let him catch it—the jackanapes!"

Emily Sarah Holt

"I did not let him catch me, Mrs Jane," answered Phoebe, with some dignity.

"That's right!" said Mrs Jane, decidedly. "That bundle of velvet and braid would never have made any way with me, when I was your age, my dear. Why, any mantua-maker could cut him out of snips, and have some stuff left over."

"He is of very good family, my dear Mrs Jane," observed Lady Betty; "at least, if I take you rightly in supposing you allude to Mr Welles."

"More pity for the family!" answered Mrs Jane. "Glad I'm not his mother. Ruin me to keep, him in order. Cost a fortune in whip-leather. How's Mrs Rhoda?"

"She is very well, I thank you, Madam."

"Is she crying out her eyes over that piece of fiddle-faddle?"

"I think she has finished for the present," replied Phoebe, rather drily.

"Just you tell her he's been making up to you. Best thing you can do. Cure her sooner than anything else."

"Mrs Phoebe, my dear, may I beg of you to do me the favour to let Madam know that my niece, my Lady Delawarr, is much disordered in her health?"

"Certainly, my Lady Betty; I am grieved to hear it."

"Very much so, as 'tis feared; and Sir Richard hath asked me thither to visit her, and see after matters a little while she is laid by. I purpose to go thither this next week, but I would not do so without paying my respects to Madam, for which honour I trust to wait on her to-morrow. Indeed, my dear—and if you will mention it to Madam, you will do me a service—Sir Richard's letter is not without some importunity that should my niece be laid aside for any time, as her physician fears, I would remove altogether, and make my home with them."

"Indeed, Madam, I will tell my mother all about it."

"I thank you, my dear; 'twill be a kindness. Of course, I would not like to leave without Madam's concurrence."

"That you will have," quietly said Mrs Dorothy.

"Indeed, so I hope," returned Lady Betty. "I dare say Mrs Phoebe here at least does not know that when my nephew Sir Richard was young, after his mother died—my poor sister Penelope—he was bred up wholly in my care, so that he looks on me rather as his mother than his aunt, and 'tis but natural that his thoughts should turn to me in this trouble."

"You must have been a young aunt, my Lady Betty," remarked Mrs Dorothy.

"Truly, but twelve years elder than my nephew," said Lady Betty, with a smile.

"Clarissa would have told us that, without waiting to be asked," laughed Mrs Jane. "How are the girls, my Lady Betty?"

"Very well, as I hear. You know, I guess, that Betty is engaged in marriage?"

"So we heard. To Sir Charles Rich, is it not?"

"The same. But maybe you have not heard of Molly's conquest?" asked Lady Betty, with an amused little laugh.

"What, is Mrs Molly in any body's chains?"

"Indeed, I guess not, Mrs Jane," replied Lady Betty, still laughing. "I expect my friend Mr Thomas Mainwaring is in Molly's chains, if chains there be."

"Eh, she'll lead him a weary life!" said Mrs Jane.

"Let us hope she will sober down," answered Lady Betty. "I am not unwilling to allow there hath of late been room for improvement. Yet is there some good in Molly, as I think."

Phoebe remembered Molly's assistance in the matter of Mr Edmundson, and thought it might be so.

"Well, and what of Mrs Gatty?"

"Ah, poor maid! She, at least, can scarce hope to be happy, her disfigurement is so unfortunate."

"I must needs ask your pardon, my Lady Betty, but I trust that is not the case," said Mrs Dorothy, with a gentle smile. "Sure, happiness doth not depend on face nor figure?"

"The world mostly reckons so, I believe," answered Lady Betty, with a responsive smile. "Maybe, we pick up such words, and use them, in something too heedless a manner."

"I am mightily mistaken if Mrs Gatty do not prove the happiest of the three," was Mrs Dorothy's reply.

Mrs Dorothy rose to go home, and Phoebe took leave at the same time. She felt tired and harassed, and longed for the rest of a little quiet talk with her old friend.

"And how doth Mrs Rhoda take this, my dear?" was the old lady's first question, when Phoebe had poured out her story.

"She seemed very much troubled at first, and angry; but I fancy she is getting over it now."

"Which most?—troubled or angry?"

"I think—after a few minutes, at least—more angry."

"Then she will quickly recover. I do not think she loved him, Phoebe. She liked him, I have no doubt: and she flattered herself that he loved her; but if she be more angry than hurt, that shows that her pride suffers rather than her love. At least," said Mrs Dorothy, correcting herself, "I mean it looks so. Who am I, that I should judge her?"

"I wanted it to do her some good, Mrs Dolly. It seems hard to have the suffering, and not get the good."

"'Tis not easy for men to tell what does good, and when. We cannot as concerns ourselves; how then shall we judge for others?"

"I wonder what Rhoda will do now?" suggested Phoebe, after a minute's silence.

She looked up, and saw an expression, which the mixture of pity and amusement, on Mrs Dorothy's lips. The amusement died away, but the pity remained and grew deeper.

"Can you guess, Mrs Dolly?"

Emily Sarah Holt

"'Lord, and what shall this man do?' You know the answer, Phoebe."

"Yes, I know: but—Mrs Dorothy, would you not like to know the future?"

"Certainly not, dear child. I am very thankful for the mist which my Father hath cast as a veil over my eyes."

"But if you could see what would come, is it not very likely that there would not be some things which you would be glad and relieved to find absent?"

"Very likely. The things of which we stand especially in fear often fail to come at all. But there would be other things, which I should be very sorry to find, and much astonished too."

"I wonder sometimes, what will be in my life," said Phoebe, dreamily.

"That which thou needest," was the quiet answer.

"What do I need?" asked Phoebe.

"To have thy will moulded after God's will."

"Do you think I don't wish God's will to be done, Mrs Dorothy?"

Mrs Dorothy smiled. "I quite believe, dear child, thou art willing He should have His way with respect to all the things thou dost not care about."

"Mrs Dorothy!"

"My dear, that is what most folks call being resigned to the will of God."

"Mrs Dolly, why do people always talk as though God's will must be something dreadful? If somebody die, or if some accident happen, they say, 'Ah, 'tis God's will, and we must submit.' But when something pleasant comes, they never say it then. Don't you think the pleasant things are God's will, as well as the disagreeable ones?"

"More so, Phoebe. 'In all our affliction, He is afflicted.' 'He doth not afflict willingly, nor grieve the children of men.' Pleasant things are what He loves to give us; bitter things, what He needs must."

"Then why do people talk so?" repeated Phoebe.

"Ah, why do they?" said Mrs Dorothy. "Man is always wronging God. Not one of us all is so cruelly misunderstood of his fellows as all of us misunderstand Him."

"Yet He forgives," said Phoebe softly: "and sometimes we don't."

"He is always forgiving, Phoebe. The inscription is graven not less over the throne in Heaven than over the cross on earth,—'This Man receiveth sinners.'"

There was a pause of some minutes; and as Phoebe rose to go, Mrs Dorothy said,—

"I will tell you one thing I have noted, child, as I have gone through life. Very often there has been something looming, as it were, before me that I had to do, or thought I should have to bear,—and in the distance and the darkness it took a dread shape, and I looked forward to it with terror. And when it has come at last, it has often—I say not always, but often—proved to be at times a light and easy cross, even at times an absolute pleasure. Again, there hath often been something in the future that I have looked forward to as a great good and delight, which on its coming hath turned out a positive pain and evil. 'Tis better we should not know the future, dear Phoebe. Our Father knows every step of the way: is not that enough? Our Elder Brother hath trodden every step, and will go with us through the wilderness. Perfect wisdom and perfect love have prepared all things. Ah, child, thy fathers were wise men to sing as they sang—

"'Mon sort n'est pas a plaindre,
Il est a desirer;
Je n'ai plus rien a craindre,
Car Dieu est mon Berger.'"

"But, Mrs Dolly—I suppose it can't be so, yet—it does seem as if there were some things in life which the Lord Jesus did not go through."

"What things, my dear?"

"Well, we never read of His having any kind of sickness for one thing."

"Are you sure of that? 'Himself took our infirmities, and bare our sicknesses,' looks very like the opposite. You and I have no idea, Phoebe, how He spent thirty out of thirty-three years of His mortal life. He may—mind, I don't say it was so, for I don't know—but He may have spent much of them in a sick chamber. He was 'in *all* points tempted like as we are.' My father used to tell me that the word there rendered 'tempted' signifies not only temptations of Satan, but trials sent of God."

"But—He was never a woman, Mrs Dolly."

"And therefore cannot feel for a woman as though He had been,—is that thy meaning, dear? Nay, Phoebe, I believe He was the only creature that ever dwelt on earth in whom were the essential elements both of man and woman. He took His flesh of the woman only. The best part of each was in Him,—the strength and intelligence of the man, the love and tenderness of the woman. 'Tis modish to say women are tender, Phoebe; more modish than true. Many are soft, but few are tender. But He was tenderness itself."

"I don't think women always are tender," said Phoebe.

"My dear," said Mrs Dorothy, "you may laugh at me, but I am very much out of conceit with my own sex. A good woman is a very precious thing, Phoebe; the rather since 'tis so rare. But an empty, foolish, frivolous woman is a sad, sad sight to see. Methinks I could scarce bear with such, but for four words that I see, as it were, graven on their brows,— 'For whom Christ died.'"

"Very good!" said Mrs Latrobe. "I will not conceal from you, Phoebe, that I am extreme gratified with this decision of Lady Betty. I trust she will carry it out."

Phoebe felt a good deal surprised. Lady Betty had been the only inmate of the Lodge whose society her mother had apparently cared to cultivate, and yet she expressed herself much pleased to hear of her probable departure. She remembered, too, that Mrs Dorothy had expected Mrs Latrobe's assent. To herself it was a mystery.

Mrs Latrobe gave no explanation at the time. She went at once to another part of the subject, informing Phoebe that she had asked Betty and Molly Delawarr on a visit. Gatty had been invited also, but had declined to leave her mother in her present condition. Phoebe received this news with some trepidation. Had it been Betty alone, she would not have minded; for she thought her very good-natured, and could not understand Rhoda's expressed dislike to her. But Molly!—Phoebe tried to remember that Molly had done one kind action, and hoped she would be on her best behaviour at White-Ladies. Mrs Latrobe went on to say that she wished Phoebe to share her room with Betty, and would put Rhoda and Molly in another. But when Phoebe ventured to ask if Rhoda might not retain the room which she knew her to prefer, and Phoebe herself be the one to change, Mrs Latrobe refused to entertain the proposition.

"No, my dear, certainly not. You forget your station, Phoebe. You are the daughter of this house, not your cousin. You must not be thinking of how things were. They have changed. I could not think of allowing Rhoda to have the best chamber. Besides, she has got to come down, and she had best know it at once."

"What do you mean, Madam, if you please?"

"What do I mean? Why, surely you have some sense of what is proper. You don't fancy she could continue to live here, do you? If she had married Mr Welles, I should have said nothing against her staying here till her marriage—of course, if it were a reasonable time; but now that is all over. She must go."

"Go!" gasped Phoebe. "Go whither, Madam?"

"I shall offer her the choice of two things, my clear. She can either go to service, in which case I will not refuse to take the trouble to look out a service for her—I am wishful to let her down gently, and be very good to her; or, if she prefer that, she may have my Lady Betty's house as soon as she is gone. Have you any idea which she will choose?"

"Service! The Maidens' Lodge! Rhoda!"

"My dear Phoebe, how very absurd you are. What do you mean by such foolish ejaculations? Rhoda will be uncommonly well off. You forget she has the interest of her money, and she has some good jewellery; she may make a decent match yet, if she is wise. But in the meantime, she must live somehow. Of course I could not keep her here—it would spoil your prospects, simpleton! She has a better figure than you, and she has more to say for herself. You must not expect any body to look at you while she is here."

"Oh, never mind that!" came from the depth of Phoebe's heart.

"But, my dear, I do mind it. I must mind it. You do not understand these things, Phoebe. Why, I do believe, with a very little encouragement—which I mean him to have—Mr Welles himself would offer for you."

"That is over, Madam."

"What is over? Phoebe! what do you mean? Has Mr Welles really spoken to you?"

"Yes, Madam."

"When, my dear?" asked Mrs Latrobe, in a tone of deep interest.

"This afternoon, Madam!"

"That is right! I am so pleased. I was afraid he would want a

Emily Sarah Holt

good deal of management. And you've no more notion how to manage a man than that parrot. I should have to do it all myself."

"I beg your pardon, Madam," said Phoebe, with some dignity; "I gave him an answer."

"Of course, you did, my dear. I am only afraid—sometimes, my dear Phoebe, you let your shyness get the better of you till you seem quite silly—I am afraid, I say, that you would hardly speak with becoming warmth. Still—"

"I think, Madam, I was as warm as you would have wished me," said Phoebe, drily.

"Oh, of course, there is a limit, my dear," said Mrs Latrobe, bridling. "Well, I am so glad that it is settled. 'Tis just what I was wishing for you."

"I fear, Madam, you misconceive me," said Phoebe, looking up, "and 'tis settled the other way from what you wished."

"Child, what can you mean?" asked Mrs Latrobe, with sudden sharpness. "You never can have refused such an excellent offer? What did you say to Mr Welles?"

"I sent him away, and told him never to come near me again." Phoebe spoke with warmth enough now.

"Phoebe, you must be a lunatic!" burst from her mother. "I could not have believed you would be guilty of such supreme, unpardonable folly!"

"Sure," said Phoebe, looking up, "you would never have had me marry a man whom I despised in my heart?"

"Despised! I protest, Phoebe, you are worse and worse. What do you mean by saying you despise Mr Welles? A man of excellent manners and faultless taste, of good family, with an estate of three thousand a year, and admirable prospects when his old uncle dies, who is nearly seventy now—why, Phoebe, you must be a perfect fool! I am amazed at you beyond words."

There was a light in Phoebe's eyes which was beyond Mrs Latrobe's comprehension.

"Mother!" came from the girl's lips, with a soft intonation— "Father would not have asked me to do that!"

"Really, my dear, if you expect that I am to rule myself by your father's notions, you expect a great deal too much. He was not a man of the world at all—"

"He was not!"

"Not in the least!—and he had not the faintest idea what would be required of you when you came to your present position. Don't quote him, I beg of you!—Well, really, Phoebe—I don't know what to do now. I wish I had known of it! Still I don't see, if he were determined to speak to you, how I could have prevented you from making such a goose of yourself. I do wish he had asked me! I should have accepted him at once for you, and not given you the chance to refuse. What did you say to him? Is it quite hopeless to try and win him back?"

"Quite," said Phoebe, shortly.

"But I want to know exactly what you said."

"I told him I believed he wanted the estate, and not me; and that after behaving to my cousin as he did, he did not need to expect to get either it or me."

"Phoebe! what preposterous folly!" said Mrs Latrobe. "Well, child, you are a fool—that's as plain as a pikestaff; but—"

"You're a fool!" came in a screech from the parrot's cage, followed by a burst of laughter.

"But 'tis no use crying over spilt milk. If we have lost Mr Welles, we have lost him; and we must try for some one else. Oh dear, how hot it is! Phoebe, I wonder when you will have any sense. I do beseech you, my dear, never to play the same game with anyone else."

"I hope, Mother," said Phoebe, gravely, "that I shall never have occasion."

"What a lot of geese!" said the parrot.

CHAPTER TWELVE

ENDS IN THE MAIDENS' LODGE

"Mother, Mother, up in Heaven,
Stand up on the jasper sea,
And be witness I have given
All the gifts required of me."

Elizabeth Barrett Browning.

"Before these young gentlewomen come, Rhoda, I want a word with you."

"Yes, Madam."

"I am sure, my dear, that you have too much wit to object to what I am about to say."

Rhoda had learned to dread this beginning, as it was generally the prelude to something disagreeable. But she was learning, also, to submit to disagreeable things. She only said, meekly, "Yes, Madam."

"I suppose, my dear, you will have felt, like a maid of some parts and spirit as you are, that your dwelling any longer with me and Phoebe in this house would not be proper."

Emily Sarah Holt

"Not be proper!" Rhoda's cheek blanched. She had never recognised anything of the kind. Was she not only to lose her fortune, but to be turned out of her home? When would her calamities come to an end? "Not proper, Aunt Anne!—why not?"

This was not altogether an easy question to answer with any reason but the real one, which last must not be told to Rhoda. Mrs Latrobe put on an air of injured astonishment.

"My dear!—sure, you would not have me tell you that? No, no!—your own good parts, I am certain, must have assured you. Now, Rhoda, I wish, so far as is possible, to spare you all mortification. If you consider that it would be easier to you to support your altered fortunes elsewhere, I am very willing to put myself to some trouble to obtain for you a suitable service; or if, on the other hand, you have not this sensibility, then my Lady Betty's cottage is at your disposal when she leaves it. The time that these young gentlewomen are here will be enough to think over the matter. When they go, I shall expect your answer."

Had Phoebe wished to tell out to Rhoda a recompense of distress equivalent to every annoyance which she had ever received from her, she could have wished for no revenge superior to that of this moment. For her, who had all her life, until lately, looked forward to dispensing her favours as the Queen of Cressingham, to be offered apartments in the Maidens' Lodge as an indigent gentlewoman, was in her eyes about the last insult and degradation which could be inflicted on her. She went white and red by turns; she took up the hem of her apron, and began to plait it in folds, with as much diligence as though it had been a matter of serious importance that there should be a given number of plaits to an inch, and all of the same width to a thread. Still she did not speak.

Mrs Latrobe required no words to inform her of what was passing in Rhoda's mind. But she forestalled any words which might have come, by an affectation of misunderstanding her.

"You see, my dear Rhoda," she said, in a would-be affectionate tone, "I am bound to do all I can for my only sister's only child. I would not do you so much injury as to suppose you insensible to the kindness I have shown you. Indeed, if you had been something younger, and had wished to learn any trade, I would willingly have paid the premium with you. And 'tis no slight matter, I can assure you. Eighty pounds would have been the least for which I could have put you with a milliner or mantua-maker, to learn her trade. But, however, 'tis no good talking of that, for you are a good nine years too old. So there is nothing before you but service, without you marry, or to take my Lady Betty's house. Now, my dear, you may go and divert yourself; we will not talk of this matter again till the young gentlewomen have ended their visit."

And with a nod of dismissal, Mrs Latrobe rose and passed out of the room, evidently considering her duties exceeded by her merits, and leaving Rhoda too stunned for words.

Trade, indeed! If there could be a deeper depth than the Maidens' Lodge, it was trade, in Rhoda's eyes. Domestic service was incomparably more respectable and honourable. As to matrimony, which her aunt had, as it were, flung into the scales as she passed, Rhoda's heart was still too sore to think of it.

An hour later brought Betty and Molly.

"How do you, Rhoda, dear?" inquired the former, kindly.

"Well!—got over it, Red Currants?" interrogated Molly.

"Over what, I beg?" said Rhoda, rather haughtily.

Molly sang her answer:—

> "'I lost my looks, I lost my health,
> I lost my wit—my love kept true;
> But one fine day I lost my wealth,
> And, presto! off my lover flew.'

"Isn't that about it, old Tadpole?"

"Your's hasn't," retorted Rhoda, carrying the attack into the enemy's country.

"No; I haven't lost my wealth yet," said Molly, gravely for her.

"Who told you?" whispered Phoebe.

"O Gemini! isn't that a good jest?" responded Molly, not at all in a whisper. "'Who told me?'—just as if three hundred and sixty-five people hadn't told me. Told me more jokes than one, too, Mrs Phoebe Latrobe; told me how *you* sent off Master Marcus with all the starch washed out of him. Got-up Marcus in the rough dry—O Gemini!" and Molly almost shrieked with laughter. "Poor wretch! Hasn't had the heart to powder himself since. And she told him to his face he wanted the guineas.—Oh how jolly! Wouldn't I have given a pretty penny to see his face! Phoebe, you're tip-top."

"What on earth are you talking about?" asked Rhoda, with something of her old sharp manner.

"Talking about your true and constant lover, my charmer,"

said Molly. "His heart was broken to bits by losing—your money; so he picked up the pieces, and pasted them together, and offered the pretty little thing to your cousin, as the nearest person to you. But she, O cruel creature! instead of giving him an etiquet of admission to her heart, what does she but come down on the wretch's corns with a blunderbuss, and crush his poor pasted heart into dust. Really—"

"Molly, my dear!" said Betty, laughing. "Does a man's heart lie in his corns?"

"If you wish to know, Mrs Betty Delawarr, the conclusions to which I have come on that subject," replied Molly, in her gravest mock manner, "they are these. Most men haven't any hearts. They have pretty little ornaments, made of French paste, which do instead. They get smashed about once in six months, then they are pasted up, and nobody ever knows the difference. There isn't much, when 'tis nicely done."

"Pray, Molly, how many women have hearts?"

"Not one among 'em, present company excepted."

"Oh, Molly, Molly!" said Betty, still laughing. "I thank you, in the name of present company," added Rhoda; but there was a glitter in her eyes which was not mirth.

"Now, Red Gooseberries (rather sour just now), you listen to me," said Molly. "If you have got a heart (leave that to you!) don't you let it waste away for that piece of flummery. There's Osmund Derwent breaking his for you, and I believe he has one. Take him—you'll never do better; and if I tell you lies for the rest of my life, I've spoken truth this time.— Now, Fib, aren't you going to show such distinguished visitors into the parlour?"

"Oh, I beg your pardon!" exclaimed Phoebe; "I was listening to you."

"Madam, I thank you for the compliment," and, with a low courtesy, Molly gave her sister a push before her into the presence of Mrs Latrobe.

"Phoebe, come here!" cried Rhoda, in a hoarse whisper, drawing her cousin aside into one of the deep recessed windows of the old hall, once the refectory of the Abbey. "Tell me, did Marcus Welles offer to you?"

"Yes," said Phoebe, and said no more. "And you refused him?"

"Why, Rhoda, dear! Yes, of course."

"Not for my sake, I hope. Phoebe, I would not marry him now, if he came with his hat full of diamonds."

"Make your mind easy, dear. I never would have done."

"Do you know, Phoebe, Aunt Anne has offered to put me in the Maidens' Lodge?"

"She talked of it," said Phoebe, pitifully.

"I am not going there," responded Rhoda, in a decisive tone. "I'll go to service first. Perhaps, I can come down so much, away from here; but to do it here, where I thought to be mistress!—no, I could not stand that, Phoebe."

"I am sorry you have to stand any of it, dear Rhoda."

"You are a good little thing, Fib; I could not bear you to pity me if you were not. If Aunt Anne had but half your—"

"Phoebe, where are you? Really, my dear, I am quite shocked at your negligence! Carry the young gentlewomen up to their chambers, and let Rhoda wait on them. I take it extreme ill you should have left them so long. Do, my dear, remember your position!"

Remember her position! Phoebe was beginning to wish heartily that she might now and then be permitted to forget it.

The four girls went upstairs together.

"I say, Fib, did you ever shoot a waterfall in a coble?" inquired Molly.

Phoebe felt safe in a negative.

"Because I've heard folks say who have, that 'tis infinitely pleasant, when you come alive out of it; but then, you see, there's a little doubt about that."

"I don't understand you, Mrs Molly."

"No, my dear, very like you don't. Well, you'll find out when you've shot 'em. You're only a passenger; no blame to you if you don't come out alive."

"Who's rowing, Molly?" asked Rhoda.

"Somebody that isn't used to handling the oars," said Molly. "And if she don't get a hole stove in—Glad 'tis no concern of mine!"

"How does Gatty now?" asked Rhoda.

"O she is very well, I thank you," replied Betty.

"Is she promised yet?"

"Dear, no," said Betty, in a pitying tone.

"Rank cruelty, only to think on it," said Molly. "She'll just come in, as pat as vinegar to lettuce, to keep you company in the Maidens' Lodge, my beloved Rhoda."

Rhoda's lip trembled slightly, but she asked, quietly enough—

"Which is the vinegar?"

Molly stood for a moment with her head on one side, contemplating Rhoda.

"Been putting sugar to it, Fib, haven't you? Well, 'tis mighty good stuff to cure a cough."

"Phoebe," said her mother that evening, when prayers were over, "I wish to speak with you in my chamber before you go to yours."

Phoebe obeyed the order with a mixture of wonder and trepidation.

"My dear, I have good news for you. I have chosen your husband."

"Mother!"

"Pray, why not, my dear? 'Tis an ingenious young man, reasonable handsome, and very suitable for age and conditions. I have not yet broke the matter to him, but I cannot doubt of a favourable answer, for he hath no fortune to speak of, and is like to be the more manageable, seeing all the money will come from you. You met with him, I believe, at Delawarr Court. His name is Derwent. I shall not write to him while these young gentlewomen are here, but directly they are gone: yet I wish to give you time to become used to it, and I name it thus early."

Phoebe felt any reply impossible.

"Good-night, my dear. I am sure you will like Mr Dement."

Phoebe went back along the gallery like one walking in a dream. How was this tangled skein ever to be unravelled? Had she any right to speak? had she any to keep silence? And a cry of "Teach me to do *Thy* will!" went up beyond the stars. "I don't know what is right," said Phoebe, plaintively, to her own heart. "Lord, Thou knowest! Make Thy way plain before my face," It seemed to her that, knowing what she did, there would be one thing more terrible than a refusal from Mr Derwent, and that would be acceptance. It seemed impossible to pray for either. She could only put the case into God's hands, with the entreaty of Hezekiah: "O Lord, I am oppressed: undertake for me."

It did not make the matter any easier that, a few days later, Rhoda said suddenly, when she and Phoebe were alone, "Do you remember that Mr Derwent who was at Delawarr Court?"

"Yes," said Phoebe, and said no more.

"Betty tells me she thought he had a liking for me."

Phoebe was silent. Would the actual question come?

"I wonder if it was true," said Rhoda.

Still Phoebe went on knitting in silence, with downcast eyes.

"I almost begin, Phoebe, to wish it had been, do you know? I liked him very well. And—I want somebody to care for *me*."

"Yes, poor dear," said Phoebe, rising hurriedly. "Excuse me, I must fetch more wool."

And she did not seem to hear Rhoda call after her—

"Why, Phoebe, here's your wool—a whole ball!"

"Pretty kettle of fish!" screamed the parrot.

Betty and Molly had gone home. Mr Onslow had read prayers, the servants were filing out of the room, and Rhoda was lighting the candles.

"Well, my dear," asked Mrs Latrobe, looking up rather suddenly, "is your decision taken?"

"It is, Madam," readily answered her niece.

"So much the better. What is it, my dear?"

"I should prefer to go to service, if you please, Madam."

"You would!" Mrs Latrobe's tone showed surprise. "Very well: I promised you your choice. As lady's woman, I suppose?"

"If you please, Madam."

"Certainly, my dear. It shall be as you wish. Then to-morrow I will begin to look out for you. I should think I shall hear of a place in a week or two."

Rhoda made no answer, but took up her candle, and departed with merely, "Good-night, Madam."

But as Phoebe went upstairs behind her, she noted Rhoda's bowed head, her hand tightly grasping the banisters, her drowning, farewell look at the family portraits, as she passed them on her way up the corridor. At length she paused before three which hung together.

In the midst stood their grandmother, a handsome, haughty figure, taken at about the age of thirty; and on either side a daughter, at about eighteen years of age. Rhoda lifted her light first to Madam's face. She said nothing to indicate her thoughts there, but passed on, and paused for another minute before the pretty, sparkling face of Anne Latrobe. Then she came back, and raised the light, for a longer time than either, to the pale, regular, unexpressive features of Catherine Peveril. Phoebe waited for her to speak. It came at last.

"I never knew her," said Rhoda, in a choked voice. "I wonder if *they* know what is happening on earth."

"I should not think so," answered Phoebe, softly.

"Well,—I hope not!"

The hand which held the lifted light came down, and Rhoda passed into her own room, and at once knelt down to her prayers. Phoebe stood irresolute, her heart beating like a hammer. An idea had occurred to her which, if it could be carried into effect, would help Rhoda out of all her trouble. But in order to be so, it was necessary that she herself must commit—in her own eyes—an act of unparalleled audacity. Could she do it? The minute seemed an hour. Phoebe heard her mother go upstairs, and shut her door. A rapid prayer went to God for wisdom. Her resolution grew stronger. She

Emily Sarah Holt

took up her candle, stole softly downstairs, found the silver inkstand and the box of perfumed letter-paper. There were only a few words written when Phoebe had done.

"Sir,—If you were now to come hither. I thinke you wou'd win my cosen. A verie few dayes may be too late. Forgive the liberty I take.

"Yours to serve you, Phoebe Latrobe."

The letter was folded and directed to "*Mr*. Osmund Derwent, Esquire." And then, for one minute, human nature had its way, and Phoebe's head was bowed over the folded note. There was no one to see her, and she let her heart relieve itself in tears. Ay, there was One, who took note of the self-abnegation which had been learned from Him. Phoebe knew that Osmund Derwent did not love her. Yet was it the less hard on that account to resign him to Rhoda? For time and circumstances might have shown him the comparatively alloyed metal of the one, and the pure gold of the other. He might have loved Phoebe, even yet, as matters stood now. But Phoebe's love was true. She was ready to secure his happiness at the cost of her own. It was not of that false, selfish kind which seeks merely its own happiness in the beloved one, and will give him leave to be happy only in its own way. Yet, after all, Phoebe was human; and some very sorrowful tears were shed, for a few minutes, over that gift laid on the altar. Though the drops were salt, they would not tarnish the gold.

It was but for a few minutes that Phoebe dared to remain there. She wiped her eyes and forced back her tears. Then she went upstairs and tapped at Betty's door.

"There's that worriting Sue," she heard Betty say inside; and then the door was opened. "Mrs Phoebe, my dear, I ask twenty pardons; I thought 'twas that Sukey,—she always comes a-worriting. What can I do for you, my dear?"

"I want you to get that letter off first thing in the morning, Betty."

Betty turned the letter all ways, scanned the address, and inspected the seal.

"Mrs Phoebe, you'll not bear me malice, I hope. You know you're only young, my dear. Are you quite certain you'll never be sorry for this here letter?"

"'Tis not what you think, Betty," said Phoebe with a smile on her pale lips which had a good deal of sadness in it. "You are sorry for my cousin, I know. 'Twill be a kind act towards her, Betty, if you will send that letter."

Betty looked into Phoebe's face so earnestly that she dropped her eyes.

"I see," said Mrs Latrobe's maid. "I'm not quiet a blind bat, Mrs Phoebe. The letter shall go, my dear. Make your mind easy."

Yet Betty did not see all there was to be seen.

"Why, Phoebe!" exclaimed Rhoda, when she got back to the bedroom, "where have you been?"

"Downstairs."

"What had you to go down for? You forgot something, I suppose. But what is the matter with your eyes?"

"They burn a little to-night, dear," said Phoebe, quietly.

The days went on, and there was no reply to Phoebe's audacious note, and there was a reply to Mrs Latrobe's situation-hunting. She announced to Rhoda on the ninth morning at breakfast that she had heard of an excellent place for her. Lady Kitty Mainwaring the mother of Molly Delawarr's future husband, was on the look-out for a "woman." She had three daughters, the eldest of whom was the Kitty who had been at Delawarr Court. Rhoda would have to wait on these young ladies, as well as their mother. It was a most eligible situation. Mrs Latrobe, on Rhoda's behalf, had accepted it at once.

Rhoda sat playing with her tea-spoon, and making careful efforts to balance it on the edge of her cup.

"Do they know who wants it?" she asked, in a husky voice.

"Of course, my dear! You did not look I should make any secret of it, sure?"

Rhoda's colour grew deeper. It was evident that she was engaged in a most severe struggle with herself. She looked up at last.

"Very good, Aunt Anne. I will go to Lady Kitty," she said.

"My dear, I accepted the place. Of course you will go," returned Mrs Latrobe, in a voice of some astonishment.

Rhoda got out of the room at the earliest opportunity, and Phoebe followed her as soon as she could. But she found her kneeling by her bed, and stole away again. Was chastening working the peaceable fruit of righteousness in Rhoda Peveril?

Phoebe wandered out into the park, and bent her steps

towards the ruins of the old church. She sat down at the foot of Saint Ursula's image, and tried to disentangle her bewildered thoughts. Had she made a mistake in sending that letter, and did the Lord intend Rhoda to go to Lady Kitty Mainwaring? Phoebe had been trying to lift her cousin out of trouble. Was it God's plan to plunge Rhoda more deeply into it, in order that she might learn her lesson the more thoroughly, and be the more truly happy afterwards? If so, Phoebe had made a stupid blunder. When would she learn that God did not need her bungling help? Yet, poor Rhoda! How miserable she was likely to be! Phoebe buried her face in her hands, and did not see that some one had come in by a ruined window, and was standing close beside her on the grass.

"Mrs Phoebe, I owe you thanks unutterable," said a voice that Phoebe knew only too well.

Phoebe sprang up. "Have you seen her, Mr Derwent?"

"I have seen no one but you," said he, gravely.

They walked up to the house together, but there Phoebe left him and sought refuge in her bed-chamber.

"Phoebe, my dear, are you here?" said Mrs Latrobe, entering the room half an hour later. "Child, did you not hear me call? I could not think where you were, and I wished to have you come down. Why, only think!—all is changed about Rhoda, and she will not go to Lady Kitty. I am a little chagrined, I confess, on your account, my dear; however, it may be all for the best. 'Tis that same Mr Derwent I had heard of, and thought to obtain for you. Well! I am very pleased for Rhoda; 'tis quite as good, or better, than any thing she could expect; and I shall easily meet with something else for you. So now, my dear Phoebe, when she is married, and all settled—for of course, now, I shall let her stay till she marries—then, child, the coast will be clear for you. By the way, you did not care any thing for him, I suppose?—and if you had, you would soon have got over it—all good girls do. Fetch me my knotting, Phoebe—'tis above in my chamber; or, if you meet Rhoda, send her."

It was a subject of congratulation to Phoebe that one of Mrs Latrobe's peculiarities was to ask questions, and assume, without waiting for it, that the answer was according to her wishes. So she escaped a reply.

But there was one thing yet for Phoebe to bear, even worse than this.

"Phoebe, dear, dear Phoebe! I am so happy!" and Rhoda twined her arms round her cousin, and hid her bright face on Phoebe's shoulder. "He says he has loved me ever since we were at Delawarr. And I think I must have loved him, just a little bit, without knowing it, or I could not love him so much all at once now. I was trying very hard to make up my mind to Lady Kitty's service—that seemed to be what God had ordered for me; and I did ask Him, Phoebe, to give me patience, and make me willing to do His will. And only think—all the while He was preparing this for me! And I don't think, Phoebe, I should have cared for that—you know what I mean—but for you—the patient, loving way you bore with me; and I haven't been kind to you, Fib—you know I haven't. Then I dare say the troubles I've had helped a little. And Mr Derwent says he should not have dared to come but for a little letter that you writ him. I owe you all my happiness—my dear, good little Fib!"

Was it all pain she had to bear? Phoebe gave thanks that night.

Ten years had passed since Madam Furnival's death, and over White-Ladies was a cloudless summer day. In the park, under the care of a governess and nurse, half a dozen children were playing; and under a spreading tree on the lawn, with a book in her hand, sat a lady, whose likeness to the children indicated her as their mother. In two of the cottages of the Maidens' Lodge that evening, tea-parties were the order of the day. In Number Four, Mrs Eleanor Darcy was entertaining Mrs Marcella Talbot and Mrs Clarissa Vane.

Mrs Marcella's health had somewhat improved of late, but her disposition had not sustained a corresponding change. She was holding forth now to her two listeners on matters public and private, to the great satisfaction of Mrs Clarissa, but not altogether to that of Mrs Eleanor.

"Well, so far as such a poor creature as I am can take any pleasure in any thing, I am glad to see Mrs Derwent back at White-Ladies. Mrs Phoebe would never have kept up the place properly. She hasn't her poor mother's spirit and working power—not a bit. The place would just have gone to wreck if she had remained mistress there; and I cannot but think she was sensible of it."

"Well, for my part," put in Mrs Clarissa, "I feel absolutely certain something must have come to light about Madam's will, you know—which positively obliged Mrs Phoebe to give up everything to Madam Derwent. 'Tis monstrous to suppose that she would have done any such thing without being obliged. I feel as sure as if I had *seen* it."

"O my dear!" came in a gently deprecating tone from Mrs Eleanor.

"Oh, I am positive!" repeated Mrs Clarissa, whose mind

Emily Sarah Holt

possessed the odd power of forcing conviction on itself by simple familiarity with an idea. "Everything discovers so many symptoms of it. I cannot but be infinitely certain. Down, Pug, down!" as Cupid's successor, which was not a dog, but a very small monkey, endeavoured to jump into her lap.

"Well, till I know the truth is otherwise, I shall give Mrs Phoebe credit for all," observed Mrs Eleanor.

"Indeed, I apprehend Clarissa has guessed rightly," said Mrs Marcella, fanning herself. "'Tis so unlikely, you know, for any one to do such a thing as this, without it were either an obligation or a trick to win praise. And I can't think *that*,— 'tis too much."

"Nay, but surely there is some love and generosity left in the world," urged Mrs Eleanor.

"Oh, if you had had my experience, my dear," returned Mrs Marcella, working her fan more vigorously, "you would know there were no such things to be looked for in *this* world. I've looked for gratitude, I can assure you, till I am tired."

"Gratitude for what?" inquired Mrs Darcy, rather pertinently.

"Oh, for all the things one does for people, you know. They are never thankful for them—not one bit."

Mrs Darcy felt and looked rather puzzled. During the fifty years of their acquaintance, she never could remember to have seen Marcella Talbot do one disinterested kindness to any mortal being.

"They take all you give them," pursued the last-named lady,

"and then they just go and slander you behind your back. Oh, 'tis a miserable world, this!—full of malice, envy, hatred, and all uncharitableness, as the Prayer-Book says."

"The Prayer-Book does not exactly say that, I think," suggested Mrs Eleanor; "it asks that we ourselves may be preserved from such evil passions."

"I am sure I wish people were preserved from them!" ejaculated Mrs Clarissa. "The uncharitableness, and misunderstanding, and unkind words that people will allow themselves to use! 'Tis perfectly heartrending to hear."

"Especially when one hears it of one's self," responded Mrs Eleanor a little drily; adding, for she wished to give a turn to the conversation, "Did you hear the news Dr Saunders was telling yesterday? The Czar of Muscovy offers to treat with King George, but as Elector of Hanover only."

"What, he has come thus far, has he?" replied Mrs Marcella. "Why, 'tis but five or six years since he was ready to marry his daughter to the Pretender, could they but have come to terms. Sure, King George will never accept of such a thing as that?"

"I should think not, indeed!" added Mrs Clarissa. "Well, did he want a bit of sugar, then?"

Pug held out his paw, and very decidedly intimated that he did.

"Mrs Leighton wants Pug; I shall give him to her," observed his mistress. "'Tis not quite so modish to keep monkeys as it was: I shall have a squirrel."

"A bit more sugar?" asked Mrs Eleanor, addressing the

monkey. "Poor Pug!"

Next door but one, in the cottage formerly occupied by Lady Betty Morehurst, were also seated three ladies at tea. Presiding at the table, in mourning dress, sat our old friend Phoebe. There was an expression of placid content upon her lips, and a peaceful light in her eyes, which showed that whatever else she might be, she was not unhappy. On her left sat Mrs Jane Talbot, a little older looking, a little more sharp and angular; and on the right, apparently unchanged beyond a slight increase of infirmity, little Mrs Dorothy Jennings.

"What a pure snug [nice] room have you here!" said Mrs Jane, looking round.

"'Tis very pleasant," said Phoebe, "and just what I like."

"Now, my dear, do you really mean to say you like this— better than White-Ladies?"

"Indeed I do, Mrs Jane. It may seem a strange thing to you, but I could never feel at home at the Abbey. It all seemed too big and grand for a little thing like me."

"Well! I don't know," responded Mrs Jane, in that tone which people use when they make that assertion as the prelude to the declaration of a very decisive opinion,—"*I* don't know, but I reckon there's a pretty deal about you that's big and grand, my dear; and I'm mightily mistaken if Mr Derwent and Mrs Rhoda don't think the same."

"My dear Jane!" said Mrs Dorothy, with a twinkle of fun in her eyes. "Mr and Madam Derwent Furnival, if you please."

"Oh, deary me!" ejaculated Mrs Jane. "Leave that stuff to you. She can call herself Madam Peveril-Plantagenet, if she likes. Make no difference to me. Mrs Rhoda she was, and Mrs Rhoda I shall call her to the end of the chapter. Don't mean any disrespect, you know—quite the contrary. Well, I'm sure I'm very glad to see her at White-Ladies; but, Mrs Phoebe, if it could have been managed, I should have liked you too."

"Thank you, Mrs Jane, but you see it couldn't."

"Well, I don't know. There was no need for you to come down to the Maidens' Lodge, without you liked. Couldn't you have kept rooms in the Abbey for yourself, and still have given all to your cousin?"

"I'd rather have this," said Phoebe, with a smile. "I am more independent, you see; and I have kept what my grandmother meant me to have, so that, please God, I trust I shall never want, and can still help my friends when they need it. I can walk in the park, and enjoy the gardens, just as well as ever; and Rhoda will be glad to see me, I know, any time when I want a chat with her."

"I should think so, indeed!" cried Mrs Jane. "Most thankless woman in the world if she wasn't."

"Oh, don't say that! You know I could not have done anything else, knowing what Madam intended, when things came to me."

"You did the right thing, dear child," said Mrs Dorothy, quietly, "as God's children should. He knew when to put the power in your hands. If Madam Derwent had come to White-Ladies ten years ago, she wouldn't have made as good use of it as she will now. She was not ready for it. And I'm mistaken if you are not happier, Phoebe, in the Maidens' Lodge, than you ever would have been if you had kept

Emily Sarah Holt

White-Ladies."

"I am sure of that," said Phoebe. "Well, but she didn't need have come down thus far!" reiterated Mrs Jane.

"She is the servant of One who came down very far, dear Jane," gently answered Mrs Dorothy, "that we through His poverty might be rich."

"Well, it looks like it," replied Mrs Jane, with a little tell-tale huskiness in her voice. "Mrs Phoebe, my dear, do you remember my saying, when Madam died, to you and Mrs Rhoda, that I'd tell you ten years after, which I was sorry for?" Phoebe smiled an affirmative. "Well, I'm not over sorry for either of you; but, at any rate, not for *you*."

"The light has come back to thine eyes; dear child, and the peace," said old Mrs Dorothy. "Ah, folks don't always know what is the hardest to give up."

And Phoebe, looking up with startled eyes, saw that Mrs Dorothy had guessed her secret. She went to the fire for fresh water from the kettle. Her face was as calm as usual when she returned. Softly she said,—

> "'Mon sort n'est pas a plaindre,
> Il est a desirer;
> Je n'ai plus rien a craindre,
> Car Dieu est mon Berger.'"

Choose from Thousands of 1stWorldLibrary Classics By

A. M. Barnard	Booth Tarkington	Edward Everett Hale
Ada Leverson	Boyd Cable	Edward J. O'Biren
Adolphus William Ward	Bram Stoker	Edward S. Ellis
Aesop	C. Collodi	Edwin L. Arnold
Agatha Christie	C. E. Orr	Eleanor Atkins
Alexander Aaronsohn	C. M. Ingleby	Eleanor Hallowell Abbott
Alexander Kielland	Carolyn Wells	Eliot Gregory
Alexandre Dumas	Catherine Parr Traill	Elizabeth Gaskell
Alfred Gatty	Charles A. Eastman	Elizabeth McCracken
Alfred Ollivant	Charles Amory Beach	Elizabeth Von Arnim
Alice Duer Miller	Charles Dickens	Ellem Key
Alice Turner Curtis	Charles Dudley Warner	Emerson Hough
Alice Dunbar	Charles Farrar Browne	Emilie F. Carlen
Allen Chapman	Charles Ives	Emily Bronte
Alleyne Ireland	Charles Kingsley	Emily Dickinson
Ambrose Bierce	Charles Klein	Enid Bagnold
Amelia E. Barr	Charles Hanson Towne	Enilor Macartney Lane
Amory H. Bradford	Charles Lathrop Pack	Erasmus W. Jones
Andrew Lang	Charles Romyn Dake	Ernie Howard Pie
Andrew McFarland Davis	Charles Whibley	Ethel May Dell
Andy Adams	Charles Willing Beale	Ethel Turner
Angela Brazil	Charlotte M. Braeme	Ethel Watts Mumford
Anna Alice Chapin	Charlotte M. Yonge	Eugene Sue
Anna Sewell	Charlotte Perkins Stetson	Eugenie Foa
Annie Besant	Clair W. Hayes	Eugene Wood
Annie Hamilton Donnell	Clarence Day Jr.	Eustace Hale Ball
Annie Payson Call	Clarence E. Mulford	Evelyn Everett-green
Annie Roe Carr	Clemence Housman	Everard Cotes
Annonaymous	Confucius	F. H. Cheley
Anton Chekhov	Coningsby Dawson	F. J. Cross
Archibald Lee Fletcher	Cornelis DeWitt Wilcox	F. Marion Crawford
Arnold Bennett	Cyril Burleigh	Fannie E. Newberry
Arthur C. Benson	D. H. Lawrence	Federick Austin Ogg
Arthur Conan Doyle	Daniel Defoe	Ferdinand Ossendowski
Arthur M. Winfield	David Garnett	Fergus Hume
Arthur Ransome	Dinah Craik	Florence A. Kilpatrick
Arthur Schnitzler	Don Carlos Janes	Fremont B. Deering
Arthur Train	Donald Keyhoe	Francis Bacon
Atticus	Dorothy Kilner	Francis Darwin
B.H. Baden-Powell	Dougan Clark	Frances Hodgson Burnett
B. M. Bower	Douglas Fairbanks	Frances Parkinson Keyes
B. C. Chatterjee	E. Nesbit	Frank Gee Patchin
Baroness Emmuska Orczy	E. P. Roe	Frank Harris
Baroness Orczy	E. Phillips Oppenheim	Frank Jewett Mather
Basil King	E. S. Brooks	Frank L. Packard
Bayard Taylor	Earl Barnes	Frank V. Webster
Ben Macomber	Edgar Rice Burroughs	Frederic Stewart Isham
Bertha Muzzy Bower	Edith Van Dyne	Frederick Trevor Hill
Bjornstjerne Bjornson	Edith Wharton	Frederick Winslow Taylor

Friedrich Kerst
Friedrich Nietzsche
Fyodor Dostoyevsky
G.A. Henty
G.K. Chesterton
Gabrielle E. Jackson
Garrett P. Serviss
Gaston Leroux
George A. Warren
George Ade
Geroge Bernard Shaw
George Cary Eggleston
George Durston
George Ebers
George Eliot
George Gissing
George MacDonald
George Meredith
George Orwell
George Sylvester Viereck
George Tucker
George W. Cable
George Wharton James
Gertrude Atherton
Gordon Casserly
Grace E. King
Grace Gallatin
Grace Greenwood
Grant Allen
Guillermo A. Sherwell
Gulielma Zollinger
Gustav Flaubert
H. A. Cody
H. B. Irving
H.C. Bailey
H. G. Wells
H. H. Munro
H. Irving Hancock
H. R. Naylor
H. Rider Haggard
H. W. C. Davis
Haldeman Julius
Hall Caine
Hamilton Wright Mabie
Hans Christian Andersen
Harold Avery
Harold McGrath
Harriet Beecher Stowe
Harry Castlemon
Harry Coghill
Harry Houidini

Hayden Carruth
Helent Hunt Jackson
Helen Nicolay
Hendrik Conscience
Hendy David Thoreau
Henri Barbusse
Henrik Ibsen
Henry Adams
Henry Ford
Henry Frost
Henry James
Henry Jones Ford
Henry Seton Merriman
Henry W Longfellow
Herbert A. Giles
Herbert Carter
Herbert N. Casson
Herman Hesse
Hildegard G. Frey
Homer
Honore De Balzac
Horace B. Day
Horace Walpole
Horatio Alger Jr.
Howard Pyle
Howard R. Garis
Hugh Lofting
Hugh Walpole
Humphry Ward
Ian Maclaren
Inez Haynes Gillmore
Irving Bacheller
Isabel Cecilia Williams
Isabel Hornibrook
Israel Abrahams
Ivan Turgenev
J.G.Austin
J. Henri Fabre
J. M. Barrie
J. M. Walsh
J. Macdonald Oxley
J. R. Miller
J. S. Fletcher
J. S. Knowles
J. Storer Clouston
J. W. Duffield
Jack London
Jacob Abbott
James Allen
James Andrews
James Baldwin

James Branch Cabell
James DeMille
James Joyce
James Lane Allen
James Lane Allen
James Oliver Curwood
James Oppenheim
James Otis
James R. Driscoll
Jane Abbott
Jane Austen
Jane L. Stewart
Janet Aldridge
Jens Peter Jacobsen
Jerome K. Jerome
Jessie Graham Flower
John Buchan
John Burroughs
John Cournos
John F. Kennedy
John Gay
John Glasworthy
John Habberton
John Joy Bell
John Kendrick Bangs
John Milton
John Philip Sousa
John Taintor Foote
Jonas Lauritz Idemil Lie
Jonathan Swift
Joseph A. Altsheler
Joseph Carey
Joseph Conrad
Joseph E. Badger Jr
Joseph Hergesheimer
Joseph Jacobs
Jules Vernes
Julian Hawthrone
Julie A Lippmann
Justin Huntly McCarthy
Kakuzo Okakura
Karle Wilson Baker
Kate Chopin
Kenneth Grahame
Kenneth McGaffey
Kate Langley Bosher
Kate Langley Bosher
Katherine Cecil Thurston
Katherine Stokes
L. A. Abbot
L. T. Meade

L. Frank Baum
Latta Griswold
Laura Dent Crane
Laura Lee Hope
Laurence Housman
Lawrence Beasley
Leo Tolstoy
Leonid Andreyev
Lewis Carroll
Lewis Sperry Chafer
Lilian Bell
Lloyd Osbourne
Louis Hughes
Louis Joseph Vance
Louis Tracy
Louisa May Alcott
Lucy Fitch Perkins
Lucy Maud Montgomery
Luther Benson
Lydia Miller Middleton
Lyndon Orr
M. Corvus
M. H. Adams
Margaret E. Sangster
Margret Howth
Margaret Vandercook
Margaret W. Hungerford
Margret Penrose
Maria Edgeworth
Maria Thompson Daviess
Mariano Azuela
Marion Polk Angellotti
Mark Overton
Mark Twain
Mary Austin
Mary Catherine Crowley
Mary Cole
Mary Hastings Bradley
Mary Roberts Rinehart
Mary Rowlandson
M. Wollstonecraft Shelley
Maud Lindsay
Max Beerbohm
Myra Kelly
Nathaniel Hawthrone
Nicolo Machiavelli
O. F. Walton
Oscar Wilde

Owen Johnson
P.G. Wodehouse
Paul and Mabel Thorne
Paul G. Tomlinson
Paul Severing
Percy Brebner
Percy Keese Fitzhugh
Peter B. Kyne
Plato
Quincy Allen
R. Derby Holmes
R. L. Stevenson
R. S. Ball
Rabindranath Tagore
Rahul Alvares
Ralph Bonehill
Ralph Henry Barbour
Ralph Victor
Ralph Waldo Emmerson
Rene Descartes
Ray Cummings
Rex Beach
Rex E. Beach
Richard Harding Davis
Richard Jefferies
Richard Le Gallienne
Robert Barr
Robert Frost
Robert Gordon Anderson
Robert L. Drake
Robert Lansing
Robert Lynd
Robert Michael Ballantyne
Robert W. Chambers
Rosa Nouchette Carey
Rudyard Kipling
Saint Augustine
Samuel B. Allison
Samuel Hopkins Adams
Sarah Bernhardt
Sarah C. Hallowell
Selma Lagerlof
Sherwood Anderson
Sigmund Freud
Standish O'Grady
Stanley Weyman
Stella Benson
Stella M. Francis

Stephen Crane
Stewart Edward White
Stijn Streuvels
Swami Abhedananda
Swami Parmananda
T. S. Ackland
T. S. Arthur
The Princess Der Ling
Thomas A. Janvier
Thomas A Kempis
Thomas Anderton
Thomas Bailey Aldrich
Thomas Bulfinch
Thomas De Quincey
Thomas Dixon
Thomas H. Huxley
Thomas Hardy
Thomas More
Thornton W. Burgess
U. S. Grant
Upton Sinclair
Valentine Williams
Various Authors
Vaughan Kester
Victor Appleton
Victor G. Durham
Victoria Cross
Virginia Woolf
Wadsworth Camp
Walter Camp
Walter Scott
Washington Irving
Wilbur Lawton
Wilkie Collins
Willa Cather
Willard F. Baker
William Dean Howells
William le Queux
W. Makepeace Thackeray
William W. Walter
William Shakespeare
Winston Churchill
Yei Theodora Ozaki
Yogi Ramacharaka
Young E. Allison
Zane Grey